Stanley Gibbons Stamp

STAMP COLLECTING

● ● ● ● ● ● ● ● ● ● ● ● ● ● ●

HOW TO IDENTIFY STAMPS

Originally compiled by

James Watson

fully revised and updated by

Michael Briggs

● ● ● ● ● ● ● ● ● ● ●

Stanley Gibbons Ltd, London and Ringwood

Published by Stanley Gibbons Ltd
Editorial, Sales Offices and Distribution Centre:
7 Parkside, Christchurch Road, Ringwood,
Hants BH24 3SH

First Published 1983
Reprinted, with amendments, 1986
Second edition, 1988
Reprinted, with amendments 1991
Third edition, 1994
Reprinted, with new cover 1998
Fourth edition, 2005

Also in Stanley Gibbons Stamp Collecting series:
Stamp Collecting – How to Start
Stamp Collecting – Collecting By Theme
Stamp Collecting – How to Arrange and Write Up a Stamp Collection
Stamp Collecting – Philatelic Terms Illustrated
Stamp Collecting – The Stanley Gibbons Guide to Stamp Collecting

The Compiler: the late James Watson joined the staff of Stanley Gibbons in 1946 and worked in the New Issues Dept before becoming a feature writer for *Gibbons Stamp Monthly*. He retired from Gibbons in 1981. Mr Watson wrote several books on philately – most notably the *Stanley Gibbons Book of Stamps and Stamp Collecting*. He also wrote about cine photography and was an expert on picture postcards of the early 20th century.

Second and third editions revised by John Holman, Editor of *Gibbons Stamp Monthly*, 1985–88. Fourth edition revised by Michael Briggs.

Designed by Michael Briggs.

Printed in Great Britain by Brown & Son.

ISBN 0-85259-614-6

S.G. Item No. 2761

CONTENTS

INTRODUCTION

You may wonder why this little guide is necessary to help you to identify your stamps. Surely, you think, most postage stamps bear the names of the countries issuing them. It is true that many stamps can be recognised by the name of the country imprinted upon them, but the point is that the stamps of many foreign countries are not inscribed with the English names we know so well. Some are not even in the familiar Roman alphabet, and sometimes the inscriptions on a stamp bewilder the experts!

From top to bottom: Stamps of Switzerland, Japan, Austria, Scandinavia (Denmark) and Latin America (Argentine Republic)

Ideally, this guide should be used with the *Stanley Gibbons Simplified Catalogue of Stamps of the World*. This catalogue provides the location and currency of each stamp-issuing territory, often with useful historical notes, such as the date of independence.

Identification is the key to the catalogue as you must be able to recognise the country which has issued a stamp before you can look it up in the catalogue. Conversely, the catalogue is also the key to identification because it records more than 417,000 stamps with over 100,000 illustrations, and a nodding acquaintance with the pattern and style of different countries' stamps will be of great assistance to identification of your own stamps. The main elements of a stamp design which provide clues to identity are the country name, subordinate or secondary inscriptions, national emblems or symbols, such as a coat of arms or monarch's head, and the currency or face value.

'Helvetia', for example, is the Latin name for Switzerland and it is used regularly on Swiss stamps. The chrysanthemum emblem appeared on Japanese stamps from 1872 to about 1947, while the modern issues are additionally inscribed 'Nippon', which is the Japanese name for Japan. Sometimes the actual design of a stamp indicates a particular country or at least the region of its location. The heraldic eagle relates to central Europe and as a design subject it will lead (supported by the inscriptions) to the identification of the early stamps of Austria ('KKPOST' or 'KREUZER'), Germany ('Deutsches Reich' or 'Reichpost'), Poland ('Poczta Polska') and possibly Albania, Finland and Russia. Centimes and francs indicate a French-speaking country; ore and krone (or krona) are Scandinavian; centavos and pesetas or pesos appear on Spanish and Latin-American stamps.

KEY INSCRIPTIONS

By 'inscriptions' we mean all the words and figures appearing on the stamp in addition to the design. For purposes of identification the most important words are those representing the country of issue, which may appear in the normal alphabet (like our own A, B, C, …), though may be in a foreign language; in the Cyrillic or Greek alphabets; or in other alphabets and scripts such as Arabic (which looks rather like 'shorthand'), Chinese, Korean and Japanese, Hindi (the Devanagari script of India), and Urdu and Bengali (Pakistan). Urdu has many Arabic and Persian words, while Persian, with Pushtu, is also the written language of Afghanistan. Malay is the language of the natives of the Malay Archipelago and islands of South-east Asia (Malaysia) and has Arabic elements infused. The Siamese language (of the inhabitants of Thailand) is derived from a form of Sanskrit, and has affinities with Chinese. Hebrew is the official language of modern Israel, and Amharic is the official tongue of Ethiopia.

Chinese

Hebrew

Malay

Korean

Bengali and Urdu

Arabic

Hindi

Amharic

Japanese

Thai

This stamp was intended for use in the Channel Islands, but was also valid in the rest of the United Kingdom

Fortunately many of these countries additionally inscribe their stamps in the normal alphabet, while some even use the recognisable English versions, such as 'Israel' and 'Thailand'. Great Britain is the only country in the world which enjoys the privilege, granted by universal accord as the inventor of the postage stamp, of omitting the country name. Since the famous Penny Black of 1840, British stamps have borne a portrait of the reigning sovereign. New collectors will soon become familiar with the heads of Queen Victoria, King Edward VII, King George V, King Edward VIII, King George VI and our present Queen Elizabeth II, which also appear on many of the stamps of the Commonwealth territories. In recent times the head of the Queen has been shown in simplified form on GB special stamps, often just as a silhouette.

British stamps show the monarch's head instead of a country name. A silhouette is usually shown on special stamps

Some stamps without a country name

Brazil   *Finland*   *Spain*

In early days, before the Universal Postal Union was founded, other countries sometimes omitted their names. These include Austria, Bosnia and Herzegovina, Brazil, Finland, Hungary, the Papal States, Portugal, Sardinia and Spain. The early postage dues of Switzerland comprised figures of value only. On the other stamps the principal clues are the figures of value and/or the portraits depicted on them. Examples are illustrated above and others will be found on pages 39 and 40. Modern stamps of Saudi Arabia use a palm tree emblem instead of a country name.

USING THE CATALOGUE

As its name implies, the Stanley Gibbons Simplified Catalogue of Stamps of the World is extremely simple to use. The countries are arranged in alphabetical order and each country title is followed by a reference indicating the part of the main 22-part catalogue which contains the full detailed listing, and by summarised notes of the country's location, status and currency. The lists of stamps then follow in chronological order, that is, according to the dates of issue of the stamps, from the earliest to the most recent. Each issue or set is headed by an illustration which has its own number (known as the 'Type number'), and next comes the list of stamps with its descriptive heading and year of issue. If there is no such description of an event or commemoration, it can generally be assumed that the stamps are definitive or regular issues.

A page from the Stanley Gibbons Simplified Catalogue of Stamps of the World

Each stamp has its own number, by which it is known and identified by all collectors and dealers who use the catalogue, and each country has its own series of numbers. Next to the stamp number, shown in the first (left-hand) column is the Type number, but if a particular stamp is not illustrated (usually only the first stamp in a set is shown), then a dash is shown, the different designs being listed below. Blanks in this column indicate that all the stamps in the set have the same design as the illustrated stamp or type. Next again are the face values and colours of the stamps with their prices – unused (first column) and used (second column).

Official stamps, postage dues, parcel post tax stamps and similar items follow the main stamp listings.

The Tristan da Cunha stamp below has a modern look and also depicts Queen Elizabeth II in silhouette in the top right-hand corner. Reference to the catalogue tells you that the stamp is the first or lowest value in a set of 'Bird' definitives issued in 1977. There are twelve stamps in the set and the style of listing is as follows:

83 Great-winged Petrel

1977. Birds. Multicoloured.
220   1p. Type **83**
221   2p. White-faced storm petrel
222   3p. Hall's giant petrel
223   4p. Soft-plumaged petrel
224   5p. Wandering albatross
225   10p. Kerguelen petrel
226   15p. Swallow-tailed tern
227   20p. Greater shearwater
228   25p. Broad-billed prion
229   50p. Great skua
230   £1 Common diving petrel
231   £2 Yellow-nosed albatross
The 3p. to £2 designs are vert.

As all the above stamps are multicoloured there was no need to repeat the colours against each stamp, those spaces being used for the design details. A little further on in your catalogue you will find a set of 'Fishes' with a slightly different arrangement:

31 Two-spined Thornfish

1978. Fishes.
246   **31**   5p. black, brown and green
247   –   10p. black, brown and green
248   –   15p. multicoloured
249   –   20p. multicoloured
DESIGNS: 10p. Five-fingered morwong; 15p. Concha wrasse; 20p. Tristan jacopever.

Knowing the country obviously eases the task of locating a particular stamp in the catalogue – look for similarities of design, subject and style. And, of course, you will then know exactly which stamps you need to complete a set, while the detailed information about the stamps and their designs will assist you in writing-up your collection. Just browsing through the catalogue will help you enormously in getting to know the 'look' of a stamp and its various inscriptions. Most countries maintain a distinctive style of design which is easily recognizable and many of the stamps you want to identify will be illustrated. If the actual stamp is not shown you should be able to track down similar characteristics of design. Once you establish the country the rest should be straightforward. Once established, catalogue numbers are rarely changed – usually only when new stamps are added to an existing range of definitives and the lists have to be renumbered to accommodate them. The changes take effect when a new edition of a catalogue is published.

Non Postage Stamps
Collectors will frequently find 'stamps' that are not listed in the Stamps of the World *catalogue. These are usually fiscal or revenue stamps, locals, telegraph stamps or souvenir labels of one kind or another. Some information about them can be found in the 'Information for Users' section of the catalogue. Such 'stamps' are normally referred to as 'cinderellas' and can form the basis of a sideline collection.*

The Gibbons catalogue only lists stamps issued for postal purposes by official postal administrations.

THE NORMAL ALPHABET

A list of country names as they appear on stamps, subordinate inscriptions (including provisional overprints and surcharges, occupation issues and special-purpose inscriptions) and abbreviations.

This listing is designed to be used with *Stanley Gibbons Simplified Catalogue of Stamps of the World*. The names in capital letters are those of the appropriate country in that catalogue. Where items are not listed in *Stamps of the World* the country name is followed by the appropriate part number of the main Stanley Gibbons catalogue.

French Equatorial Africa

Belgian Occupation of Germany

Trieste

A. Overprint on stamps of Colombia for Avianca Air Company. COLOMBIA – Private Air Companies.

A & T. Overprint/surcharge on French Colonies 'Commerce' stamps for ANNAM AND TONGKING.

Açores. AZORES.

Admiralty Official. Overprint on British stamps 1903. GREAT BRITAIN – Official Stamps.

A.E.F. 'Afrique Equatoriale Française'. Inscription on 'Centenaire du Gabon' issue of 1938. FRENCH EQUATORIAL AFRICA.

Afghanes, Postes. AFGHANISTAN.

Africa. PORTUGUESE COLONIES, 1898. General issue.

Africa Occidental Española. SPANISH WEST AFRICA.

Africa Orientale Italiana. ITALIAN EAST AFRICA.

Afrique Equatoriale Française. FRENCH EQUATORIAL AFRICA.

Afrique Française Libre. Overprint on stamp of Middle Congo. FRENCH EQUATORIAL AFRICA.

Afrique Occidentale Française. FRENCH WEST AFRICA.

Albania. With surcharge in para currency. ITALIAN P.O.s IN THE LEVANT.

Alexandrie. ALEXANDRIA. French Post Office.

Algérie. ALGERIA.

Allemagne Duitschland. Belgian stamps overprinted for Rhineland. BELGIAN OCCUPATION OF GERMANY.

A.M.G. F.T.T. 'Allied Military Government – Free Territory of Trieste'. Overprint on Italian stamps. TRIESTE.

A.M.G. V.G. 'Allied Military Goverment – Venezia Giulia'. Overprint on Italian stamps. VENEZIA GIULIA AND ISTRIA.

A.M. Post Deutschland. GERMANY (ALLIED OCCUPATION) – Anglo-American Zone, 1945.

Amtlicher Verkehr K. Württ. Post. WURTTEMBERG – Official Stamps.

Andorre. ANDORRA (French Post Offices).

Anna(s). Surcharged on British Stamps. BRITISH POSTAL AGENCIES IN EASTERN ARABIA. Also on French stamps for FRENCH P.O.s IN ZANZIBAR.

Antananarivo, British Consular Mail. MADACASGAR (*Part 1*).

A.O. 'Afrique Orientale'. Overprint on Belgian Congo Red Cross stamps for Belgian Occupation of RUANDA-URUNDI.

AOF. 'Afrique Occidentale Française'. Overprint on French stamp. FRENCH WEST AFRICA.

A.O.I. 'Africa Orientale Italiana'. Overprint on Italian Postage Due stamps. ITALIAN EAST AFRICA.

A payer te betalen. BELGIUM – Postage Dues.

A percevoir. 'To collect'. Postage Due stamps of BELGIUM, FRANCE, GUADELOUPE, CANADA, EGYPT, MONACO.

A percevoir timbre taxe. FRENCH COLONIES – Postage Dues.

Archipel des Comores. COMORO ISLANDS.

Army Official. Overprint on British stamps, 1896–1902. GREAT BRITAIN – Official Stamps. Also overprint on Sudan stamps. SUDAN – Army Service Stamps.

Army Service. Overprint on Sudan stamps, 1906. SUDAN – Army Service Stamps.

Arriba España as part of overprint on stamps of Spain. SPAIN – Civil War issues (*Part 9*).
Assistência D.L. no. 72. Educational Tax overprint. PORTUGUESE TIMOR, 1936–37.
Aunus. Overprint on Finnish stamps. FINNISH OCCUPATION OF AUNUS.

Autopaketti. For parcels carried by road. FINLAND, 1949 onwards.
Avila por España. Overprint on stamps of Spain. SPAIN – Civil War issues (*Part 9*).
Avion Nessre Tafari. Airmail stamps. ETHIOPIA, 1931.
Avisporto Maerke. DENMARK, 1907–15 – Newspaper Stamps.
Azarbaycan. AZERBAIJAN.

B. 'Bangkok'. Overprint on Straits Settlements stamps for BRITISH POST OFFICES IN SIAM.
B. Within oval. Overprint and inscription on Railway Official stamps of BELGIUM.
B. As part of overprint/surcharge on stamps of Nicaragua. NICARAGUA – Zelaya (*Part 15*).
B.A. Eritrea, B.A. Somalia or **B.A. Tripolitania.** Overprints/surcharges on British stamps. BRITISH OCCUPATION OF ITALIAN COLONIES.
Baden. German State until 1871, listed under BADEN. French zone of occupation 1947–9, listed under GERMANY (ALLIED OCCUPATION).
Baena por España. Overprint on stamps of Spain. SPAIN – Civil War issues (*Part 9*).
Bánát Bacska. Overprint on Hungarian stamps. ROMANIAN OCCUPATION OF HUNGARY.
Bani and **lei.** Surcharges for K.u.K.Feldpost. AUSTRO-HUNGARIAN MILITARY POST – Issues for Romania.

Baranya. Overprint/surcharge on Hungarian stamps. SERBIAN OCCUPATION OF HUNGARY.
Basel, Stadt Post. Basel Town Post. SWITZERLAND – Cantonal Administrations (*Part 8*).
Bayern. BAVARIA. Now part of Germany.
B.C.A. Overprint on Rhodesian stamps for British Central Africa Protectorate. NYASALAND PROTECTORATE, 1891–95.
B.C.M. British Consular Mail. MADAGASCAR, 1884–86 (*Part 1*).
B.C.O.F. Japan 1946. 'British Commonwealth Occupation Forces'. Overprint on Australian stamps. BRITISH OCCUPATION OF JAPAN.
België/Belgique. BELGIUM. Flemish/French inscriptions.
Belgien. Overprint/surcharge on German stamps. GERMAN OCCUPATION OF BELGIUM.
Belgisch Congo. BELGIAN CONGO.
Benadir. SOMALIA, 1903–05.
Bengasi. Overprint/surcharge on Italian stamps. ITALIAN P.O.s IN THE LEVANT.
Berlin. Overprint on Allied Occupation stamps (1947) for GERMANY (WEST BERLIN).
Berlin, Notopfer. GERMANY (ALLIED OCCUPATION) – Obligatory Tax Stamp.
Berlin, Stadt. Berlin – Brandenburg. ALLIED OCCUPATION OF GERMANY – Russian Zone (*Part 7*).
Beyrouth. Overprint on Russian stamps. RUSSIAN POST OFFICES IN THE TURKISH EMPIRE (*Part 10*).
B.I.E. 'Bureau International d'Education' (International Education Office). Overprint on Swiss stamp. SWITZERLAND – International Organizations.
B L C I (one letter in each corner). BHOPAL.
B.M.A. Malaya. Overprint on Straits Settlements stamps. MALAYA – British Military Administration.
B.M.A. Eritrea, B.M.A. Somalia or **B.M.A. Tripolitania.** Overprints/surcharges on British stamps. BRITISH OCCUPATION OF ITALIAN COLONIES.
B.N.F. Castellorizo. As overprint. See O.N.F. Castellorizo.

Belgium – Railway Official

Bavaria

Belgium

Switzerland – International Organizations

Bohemia and Moravia

Bosnia and Herzegovina

Board of Education. Overprint on British stamps 1902. GREAT BRITAIN – Official Stamps.
Böhmen und Mähren. BOHEMIA AND MORAVIA. German protectorate issues.
Boka Kotorska. Overprint/surcharge on stamps of Yugoslavia. GERMAN OCCUPATION OF DALMATIA.
Bollo Postale. 'Postage Stamp'. SAN MARINO, 1877–1935.
Bosna i Hercegovina. BOSNIA AND HERZEGOVINA – Sarajevo Government. Additionally inscribed 'Hrvatska Republika (or H.R.) Herceg Bosna' – Croatian Posts.
Bosnien Hercegovina (or Herzegowina). BOSNIA AND HERZEGOVINA. Military Post.
Brasil. BRAZIL.
Braunschweig. BRUNSWICK. Now part of Germany.
British Bechuanaland. Overprint and inscription. BECHUANALAND, 1885–91.
British Central Africa. NYASALAND PROTECTORATE, 1891–1903.
British New Guinea. Former name of PAPUA.
British Occupation. Overprint/ surcharge on Russian and Batum stamps. BATUM, 1919–20.
British Somaliland. Overprint on Indian stamps for the SOMALILAND PROTECTORATE.
British South Africa Company. Former name of RHODESIA.
Brunei Darussalam. BRUNEI since 1984.
Buchanan. Registration stamp of LIBERIA 1893.
Bureau International d'Education, also with **Courrier du.** 'International Education Office'. Overprint/ inscription on Swiss stamps. SWITZERLAND – International Organizations.
Bureau International du Travail, also with **Courrier du.** 'International Labour Office'. Overprint/inscription on Swiss stamps. SWITZERLAND – International Organizations.

C. As part of overprint on stamps of Nicaragua. NICARAGUA – Zelaya (*Part 15*).
Cabo. Overprint on stamps of Nicaragua. NICARAGUA – Zelaya (*Part 15*).

Cambodia

Cabo Jubi/Cabo Juby. Overprint on stamps of Rio de Oro, Spain or Spanish Morocco. CAPE JUBY.
Cabo Verde. CAPE VERDE ISLANDS.
Cache(s). (Unit of currency). Surcharge on Postage Due stamps of France. FRENCH INDIAN SETTLEMENTS.
Calchi/Karki. Overprint on Italian stamps for Khalki. DODECANESE ISLANDS.
Calimno/Calino. Overprint on Italian stamps for Kalimnos. DODECANESE ISLANDS.
Camb. Aust. Sigillum Nov. NEW SOUTH WALES.
Cambodge. CAMBODIA.
Cameroons U.K.T.T. 'United Kingdom Trust Territory'. Overprint on Nigerian stamps. CAMEROON.
Campione, Comune de. CAMPIONE (*Part 8*).
Canal Maritime de Suez. SUEZ CANAL COMPANY (*Part 19*).
Canarias. As part of surcharge on stamps of Spain. SPAIN – Civil War issues (*Part 9*).

Caso. Overprint on Italian stamps for Kasos. DODECANESE ISLANDS.
Castellorizo/Catelloriso. CASTELROSSO.
Cavalle. CAVALLA (KAVALLA). French Post Office.
C. CH. with figure '5' on French Colonies stamps. COCHIN-CHINA.
Čechy a Morava. BOHEMIA AND MORAVIA. German protectorate issues.
C.E.F. Overprint on Indian stamps for CHINA EXPEDITIONARY FORCE; also with surcharge on German 'Kamerun' stamps for Cameroons Expeditionary Force. CAMEROON.
Cefalonia e Itaca. Part of overprint on Greek stamps. ITALIAN OCCUPATION OF CEPHALONIA AND ITHACA.

Cent (s). Also **F** for franc. Surcharges for Belgium and Northern France. GERMAN COMMANDS. Surcharges on stamps of Russia. RUSSIAN P.O.s IN CHINA.

Centesimi and **lire**. Surcharges for K.u.K. Feldpost. AUSTRO-HUNGARIAN MILITARY POST – Issues for Italy.

Centesimo (or **centesimi**) **di corona**. Surcharge on Italian stamps for AUSTRIAN TERRITORIES ACQUIRED BY ITALY.

Centimes. Surcharge on German stamps for GERMAN P.O.s IN THE TURKISH EMPIRE. Also on stamps of Austria for AUSTRO-HUNGARIAN P.O.s IN THE TURKISH EMPIRE.

Centimos. Surcharge on French stamps for FRENCH P.O.s IN MOROCCO.

Centrafricaine, République. CENTRAL AFRICAN REPUBLIC.

Česká Republika. CZECH REPUBLIC. Former part of Czechoslovakia.

Československe Armady Siberske or **Československe Vojsko Na Rusi.** CZECHOSLOVAK ARMY IN SIBERIA.

Československo(a). CZECHOSLOVAKIA.

Českých Skatu. CZECHOSLOVAKIA.

CFA 'Communaute Financielle Africaine'. Overprint/surcharge on French stamps for REUNION.

C.G.H.S. 'Commission de Gouvernement Haute Silésie'. Overprint on German Official stamps for plebiscite in UPPER SILESIA.

Chemins de Fer Spoorwegen. Railway Parcels stamps. BELGIUM.

Chiffre Tax. Postage Due stamps. FRANCE and FRENCH COLONIES. On stamps denominated in paras and piastres, TURKEY.

China. CHINA (PEOPLE'S REPUBLIC), from 1992.

China. Overprint on Hong Kong stamps for BRITISH POST OFFICES IN CHINA. Also on German stamps for GERMAN P.O.s IN CHINA.

China, Republic of. CHINA, 1913–29 and CHINA (TAIWAN), from 1953.

Chine. Overprint, surcharge and inscription for FRENCH P.O.s IN CHINA.

C.I.H.S. in circle. Overprint on German stamps for plebiscite in UPPER SILESIA.

Cilicie. CILICIA.

Cinquantenaire 24 Septembre 1853–1903 and eagle overprint on French stamps for 50th anniversary of French occupation. NEW CALEDONIA.

Cirenaica. CYRENAICA.

Città Del Vaticano. VATICAN CITY.

C.M.T. in box with value. 'Comandamentul Militar Territorial'. Surcharge on stamps of Austria. WEST UKRAINE – Romanian Occupation (*Part 10*).

Coamo. Type-set provisional. PUERTO RICO (*Part 22*).

Co. Ci. 'Commissariato Civile'. Overprint on Yugoslav stamps for the Italian Occupation of SLOVENIA.

Cocuk Esirgeme (or **C.E.**) **Kurumu.** Inscription on Child Welfare stamps of TURKEY.

Colombia. COLOMBIA. Also inscribed on stamps of PANAMA, 1887–92.

Coloniale Italiane, R.R. Poste. ITALIAN COLONIES. General issues, 1932–34.

Colonie Italiane. Overprint on Italian 'Dante' stamps of 1932 for ITALIAN COLONIES.

Colonies de l'Empire Français. FRENCH COLONIES. 'Eagle' issue, 1859.

Colonies Postes. FRENCH COLONIES. French 'Commerce' type, 1881. NOTE. French stamps without special distinction or inscription were also issued for the French Colonies up to 1877. For details see under FRANCE in the Catalogue.

Upper Silesia

Vatican City

Slovenia

Mozambique Company

Switzerland

Spain

Austrian Territories
Acquired by Italy

Comité Français de la Liberation Nationale. With 'RF' or 'République Française'. FRENCH COLONIES.
Comité International Olympique. 'International Olympic Committee'. Inscription on Swiss stamps. SWITZERLAND – International Organizations.
Comores, Archipel des. or **Republique Federale Islamique des.** COMORO ISLANDS.
Communicaciones. SPAIN.
Companhia de Mozambique. MOZAMBIQUE COMPANY.
Companhia do Nyassa. NYASSA COMPANY.
Compañia Colombiana de Navegacíon Aérea. Private Air Company stamps. COLOMBIA (*Part 20*).
Confed. Granadina. COLOMBIA, 1859.
Confœderatio Helvetica. SWITZERLAND. 'National Fete' issues, etc. 1938–52.
Congo. CONGO (BRAZZAVILLE) 1991–. CONGO (KINSHASA) 1960. On key-types of Portuguese Group – PORTUGUESE CONGO.
Congo Belge. BELGIAN CONGO.
Congo Française Gabon. GABON.
Congo Française. FRENCH CONGO.
Congo, République Démocratique du. CONGO DEMOCRATIC REPUBLIC (EX ZAIRE). CONGO (KINSHASA), 1964–71.
Congo, République du. CONGO (BRAZZAVILLE), 1959–70, 1993; CONGO (KINSHASA), 1961–64.
Congo, République Populaire du. CONGO (BRAZZAVILLE), 1970–91.
Congreso de los Diputados. SPAIN – Official Stamps, 1895.
Congreso Internacional de Ferrocarriles. Inscription on stamps of SPAIN, 1930.
Constantinopol Posta Romana. Circular overprint on Romanian stamps. ROMANIAN P.O.s IN THE TURKISH EMPIRE.
Constantinople. Overprint on stamps of Russia. RUSSIAN POST OFFICES IN THE TURKISH EMPIRE (*Part 10*).
Constantinopoli. Overprint and surcharge on Italian stamps. ITALIAN P.O.s IN THE TURKISH EMPIRE. For Constantinople.
Cordoba. ARGENTINE REPUBLIC – Cordoba (*Part 20*).

Corfu. Overprint on Italian stamps. ITALIAN OCCUPATION OF CORFU. Also overprint on Greek stamps. ITALIAN OCCUPATION OF CORFU AND PAXOS.
Corée, Postes de. KOREA, 1902–03.
Corona(e). Surcharge on Italian stamps for AUSTRIAN TERRITORIES ACQUIRED BY ITALY.
Corrientes. ARGENTINE REPUBLIC – Corrientes (*Part 20*).
Correspondencia Urgente. SPAIN – Express Letter Stamps.
Cos or **Coo.** Overprint on Italian stamps for Kos, DODECANESE ISLANDS.

Côte d'Ivoire. IVORY COAST.
Côte Française des Somalis. FRENCH SOMALI COAST.
Cour Internationale de Justice or **Cour Permanente**, etc. Overprint/ inscription on special stamps for the Court of International Justice, The Hague. NETHERLANDS – International Court of Justice.
Crete. Overprint and surcharge on French stamps. FRENCH P.O.s IN CRETE.
C.S. or **C.S.A.** CONFEDERATE STATES OF AMERICA.

Dai Nippon. Overprint/surcharge on Malayan States stamps. MALAYA (JAPANESE OCCUPATION OF).
Danmark. DENMARK.
Dansk Vestindiske Öer/Dansk Vestindien. DANISH WEST INDIES.
Dardanelles. Overprint on stamps of Russia. RUSSIAN POST OFFICES IN THE TURKISH EMPIRE (*Part 10*).
Datia. DUTTIA. A state of central India.
DBP. 'Dalni-Vostochnaya Respublika' (Far Eastern Republic). Overprint in fancy letters on stamps of Russia or Siberia. SIBERIA.
D de A. 'Departmento de Antioquia'. Inscription on issue of 1890. ANTIOQUIA.

DDR. 'Deutsche Demokratische Republik' (German Democratic Republic). GERMANY (EAST GERMANY).

Dédéagh. DEDEAGATZ.

Deficit. Overprint/inscription on Postage Due stamps. PERU.

Demokratska Federativna Jugoslavija. Overprint/surcharge on Croatian stamps. YUGOSLAVIA (Democratic Federation). Regional issues.

Denda. Inscription on Postage Due stamps of MALAYSIA.

Deutsche Besetzung Zara. Overprint on stamps of Italy. GERMAN OCCUPATION OF DALMATIA.

Deutsche Bundespost. GERMANY (FEDERAL REPUBLIC).

Deutsche Bundespost Berlin. GERMANY (WEST BERLIN).

Deutsche Demokratische Republik. GERMANY (EAST GERMANY).

Deutsche Feldpost. GERMANY. Military Fieldpost stamps, 1944.

Deutsche Flugpost/Deutsche Luftpost. GERMANY. Airmail stamps, 1919–38.

Deutsche Militär-verwaltung Kotor. Overprint/surcharge on stamps of Italy. GERMAN OCCUPATION OF DALMATIA.

Deutsche Post. GERMANY (FEDERAL REPUBLIC) and (ALLIED OCCUPATION) – British and American Zone and Russian Zone.

Deutsche Post Osten. Overprint/ surcharge on German stamps for Nazi Occupation. POLAND, 1939.

Deutsche Reichspost/Deutsches Reich. GERMANY. 'Empire' issues, 1872–87 and 1902–43.

Deutschland. GERMANY (FEDERAL REPUBLIC) from 1995.

Deutsch-Neu-Guinea. GERMAN NEW GUINEA.

Deutsch-Ostafrika. GERMAN EAST AFRICA.

Deutschösterreich. AUSTRIA. Issues of 1918–20.

Deutsch-Sudwestafrika. GERMAN SOUTH WEST AFRICA.

Dienstmarke. GERMANY. Official stamps from 1920.

Diligencia. URUGUAY. 'Mailcoach' issue of 1856.

Dios Patria Libertad. DOMINICAN REPUBLIC. Inscription on early issues.

Dios, Patria, Rey. SPAIN – Carlist issues (*Part 9*). As overprint on stamps of Spain. SPAIN – Civil War issues (*Part 9*).

DJ. Overprint on Obock stamp for DJIBOUTI, 1893.

Dollar(s). Surcharge on stamps of Russia. RUSSIAN P.O.s IN CHINA.

Dominicana, República. DOMINICAN REPUBLIC.

Donau Dampfschiffahrt Gesellshaft, Erste k.k.pr. DANUBE STEAM NAVIGATION COMPANY (*Part 2*).

D.P.R.K. 'Democratic People's Republic of Korea'. KOREA (NORTH KOREA), 1977–80.

DPR Korea. KOREA (NORTH KOREA). Issues since 1980 (stamps inscribed DPR of Korea in 1976).

Drzava S.H.S. (also **with Bosna i Hercegovina**). YUGOSLAVIA – Issues for Bosnia and Herzegovina, or Slovenia.

Drzavna Posta Hrvatska. YUGOSLAVIA – Issues for Croatia, 1918–19.

Duc. di Parma Piac. Ecc. PARMA.

Durango. As part of overprint on stamps of Spain. SPAIN – Civil War issues (*Part 9*).

Durazzo. Overprint/surcharge on Italian stamps. ITALIAN P.O.s IN THE TURKISH EMPIRE.

EA. Overprint on stamps of France. ALGERIA.

E.A.F. 'East Africa Forces'. Overprint on British stamps. BRITISH OCCUPATION OF ITALIAN COLONIES – Somalia.

East Africa and Uganda Protectorates. Listed under KENYA, UGANDA AND TANGANYIKA.

East India Postage. INDIA. Stamps of 1860. Also, surcharged with a crown and value in cents – STRAITS SETTLEMENTS first issue of 1867.

Austria

Russian POs in China

North Korea

Yugoslavia

Estonia

Ireland

Oceanic Settlements

EE. UU. De C., E.S. DEL T. 'Estados Unidos de Colombia, Estado Soberano del Tolima'. First issue of TOLIMA.

E.E.F. 'Egyptian Expeditionary Force'. Inscription on stamps of PALESTINE, 1918–22.

Eesti. ESTONIA.

Egeo. Overprint on Italian stamps. DODECANESE ISLANDS, 1912.

Egypte, Royaume d'Egypte, Postes Egyptiennes or **Poste Khedevie Egiziane.** EGYPT.

Eire. IRELAND (REPUBLIC).

Eireann, Poblacht na h. IRELAND (REPUBLIC).

Elsass. Overprint on German stamps. GERMAN OCCUPATION OF ALSACE.

Elua Keneta. 'Two Cents'. HAWAII.

E.R.I. 6d. Surcharge on 6d. stamp of ORANGE FREE STATE.

Escuelas. 'Schools'. Fiscals valid for postal use. VENEZUELA.

España or **Española.** SPAIN.

España Valencia. SPAIN – Carlist issues (*Part 9*).

Estado da India. PORTUGUESE INDIA.

Estados Unidos de Nueva Granada. COLOMBIA, 1861.

Est Africain Allemand Occupation Belge or **Duitsch Oost Afrika Belgische Bezetting** (Flemish). Overprint on Belgian Congo stamps for Belgian Occupation of RUANDA-URUNDI.

Estensi, Poste. MODENA, 1852.

Estero. 'Foreign'. Overprint on modified Italian stamps for ITALIAN P.O.s IN THE TURKISH EMPIRE.

Estland Eesti. GERMAN OCCUPATION OF ESTONIA.

Etablissements Française dans l'Inde. FRENCH INDIAN SETTLEMENTS.

Etablissements (or **Ets.**) **Française de l'Océanie.** OCEANIC SETTLEMENTS.

Etat Comorien. COMORO ISLANDS.

Etat Indépendant du Congo. BELGIAN CONGO – Independent State.

Ethiopie/Postes Ethiopiennes. ETHIOPIA.

Eupen & Malmédy. Overprint/surcharge on Belgian stamps. BELGIAN OCCUPATION OF GERMANY.

Expossicion Gral. Sevilla Barcelona. SPAIN 1929.

Fanon(s). (Unit of currency). Surcharge on Postage Due stamps of France. FRENCH INDIAN SETTLEMENTS.

Fdo. Poo. Inscription on surcharged fiscal stamps. FERNANDO POO.

Filipinas (or **Filipas**). PHILIPPINES.

Fiume Rijeka. Overprint with date 3-V-1945 and surcharge on Italian stamps. VENEZIA GIULIA AND ISTRIA – Yugoslav Occupation.

Florida. With picture of heron. URUGUAY. Air stamp of 1925.

Forces Françaises Libres Levant with Lorraine Crosses. Overprint/surcharge on Syrian and Lebanese stamps. FREE FRENCH FORCES IN THE LEVANT.

Føroyar. FAROE ISLANDS.

Franc. Surcharge on Austrian stamps. AUSTRO-HUNGARIAN P.O.s IN THE TURKISH EMPIRE.

Franc (with **Empire** or **Repub.**). FRANCE, FRENCH COLONIES.

France d'Outre-Mer. FRENCH COLONIES.

Franco. 'Helvetia' seated. SWITZERLAND, 1854.

Franco Bollo. 'Postage Stamp'. First issues of ITALY, NEAPOLITAN PROVINCES and SARDINIA. With 'Postale' added to crossed keys design, PAPAL STATES.

Francobollo di Stato. ITALY – Official Stamps.

Franco Marke. BREMEN, 1856.

Franco Scrisorei. ROMANIA, 1862.

Freimarke. 'Postage Stamp'. With portrait, PRUSSIA, 1850. With large numerals, THURN AND TAXIS.

Frimaerke (with 4 Skilling). First issue of NORWAY.

Frimaerke Kgl. Post or **Kgl. Post. Frm.** DENMARK/DANISH WEST INDIES. Kgl. or Kongeligt means 'Royal'.

G. Overprint on Cape of Good Hope stamps for GRIQUALAND WEST, 1877.

G. Overprint on stamps of CANADA for government use, 1950–63.

GAB. Overprint and surcharge on French Colonial stamp for GABON, 1886.

Gabonaise, République. GABON.

G.E.A. 'German East Africa'. Overprint on Kenya and Uganda stamps for British Occupation of TANGANYIKA.

Gen.-Gouv. Warschau. Overprint on German stamps. GERMAN OCCUPATION OF POLAND.

General Gouvernement. POLAND – German Occupation, 1940–44.

Genève, Post de. Geneva. SWITZERLAND – Cantonal Administrations (*Part 8*).

Georgie (La) or **République Georgienne.** GEORGIA, 1919–21.

Gerusalemme. Overprint/surcharge on Italian stamps for Jerusalem. ITALIAN P.O.s IN THE TURKISH EMPIRE.

G et D (or **G & D**). Overprint/surcharge on Guadeloupe stamps for Guadeloupe and Dependencies. GUADELOUPE.

G.F.B. 'Gaue Faka Buleaga' (On Government Service). Overprint on Tonga stamps, 1893. TONGA – Official Stamps.

G.K.C.A. Within dotted circle. Overprint on Yugoslav stamps for the Carinthian plebiscite, 1920. YUGOSLAVIA.

G.N.R. 'Guardia Nazionale Repubblicana'. Overprint on stamps of Italy. ITALY – Italian Social Republic.

Golfo de Guinea, Territorios (or **Terrs.**) **del.** Overprint on Spanish stamps for SPANISH GUINEA.

Govt. Parcels. Overprint on British stamps, 1883–1902. GREAT BRITAIN – Official Stamps.

G.P.E. Overprint/surcharge on French Colonies for GUADELOUPE.

Graham Land Dependency of. FALKAND ISLANDS DEPENDENCIES.

Granadina, Confed. COLOMBIA, 1859.

Grande Comore. GREAT COMORO.

Grand Liban. 'Greater Lebanon'. LEBANON, 1924–26.

Grenada Carriacou & Petite Martinique. GRENADINES OF GRENADA.

Grenville. Registration stamp of LIBERIA, 1893.

G.R.I. 'Georgius Rex Imperator'. Overprint and surcharge in British currency on stamps and registration labels of German New Guinea and Marshall Islands during Australian Occupation of NEW GUINEA; also on German Cameroons stamps for New Zealand administration of SAMOA.

G.R. Post Mafia. Overprint on stamps of Indian Expeditionary Force. TANGANYIKA.

Grønland. GREENLAND.

Grossdeutsches Reich. GERMANY. Issues of 1943–45.

Gruzija. GEORGIA.

Guiné. PORTUGUESE GUINEA.

Guinea Ecuatorial, Republica de. EQUATORIAL GUINEA.

Guinea Española. SPANISH GUINEA.

Guiné-Bissau. GUINEA-BISSAU.

Guinée, also **Republique de.** FRENCH GUINEA.

Guinée, République de. GUINEA.

Gultig 9. Armee. Overprint on stamps of Germany. GERMAN OCCUPATION OF ROMANIA.

Guyane Française. FRENCH GUIANA.

G.W. Overprint on Cape of Good Hope stamps for GRIQUALAND WEST. 1877.

Harper. Registration stamp of LIBERIA, 1893.

Haut (or **Ht.**) **Sénégal-Niger.** UPPER SENEGAL AND NIGER.

Haute-Silésie. UPPER SILESIA. Plebiscite issues, 1920–22.

Haute-Volta. UPPER VOLTA.

H.E.H. The Nizam's Government/ Silver Jubilee. HYDERABAD.

Hellas. GREECE.

Helvetia. SWITZERLAND.

Herzogth. (or **Herzogthum**) **Holstein** or **Schleswig.** SCHLESWIG-HOLSTEIN.

H.H. Nawab Shah Jahan Begam. BHOPAL.

Poland

Italy – Italian Social Republic

Georgia

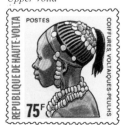

Upper Volta

Croatia

Venezuela

Iceland

Venezia Giulia and Istria

Finnish Occupation of Eastern Karelia

H.I. (& U.S.) Postage. 'Hawaiian Islands'. HAWAII.

Holkar State. INDORE.

Homenaje General Varela. As part of overprint on stamps of Spain. SPAIN – Civil War issues (*Part 9*).

Hrvatska (with **ND, Nezavisna Drzava** or **Republika**). CROATIA.

Hrvatska (with **SHS, Drzavna Posta** or **DRZ SHS**). YUGOSLAVIA – Issues for Croatia, 1918–19.

Hrvatska Republika (with **Bosna i Hercegovina**). BOSNIA AND HERZGOVINA – Croatian Posts.

Hrzgl. Frm(rk). SCHLESWIG-HOLSTEIN.

I.B. 'Irian Barat'. WEST IRIAN. Now part of Indonesia.

I.E.F. Overprint on Indian stamps for INDIAN EXPEDITIONARY FORCES.

I.E.F. 'D'. Overprint/surcharge in annas on Turkish fiscal stamps for Indian forces in Mesopotamia. MOSUL.

Ierusalem. Overprint on stamps of Russia. RUSSIAN POST OFFICES IN THE TURKISH EMPIRE (*Part 10*).

Ile de la Réunion. REUNION.

Ile Rouad. Overprint and surcharge on French stamps for ROUAD ISLAND (ARWAD).

Iles Wallis et Futuna. WALLIS AND FUTUNA ISLANDS.

Imperial British East Africa Company. BRITISH EAST AFRICA.

Imperio Colonial Portugues. Postage Due stamps. PORTUGUESE COLONIES.

Impuesto (or **Impto.**) **de Guerra.** SPAIN – War Tax Stamps.

India/India Portugueza (or **Port.** or **Portugesa**), **Estado da.** PORTUGUESE INDIA.

Inde Française (or **Fçaise**). FRENCH INDIAN SETTLEMENTS.

Independence 11th November 1965. Overprint on stamps of Southern Rhodesia. RHODESIA.

Indo-Chine/Indochine. INDO-CHINA.

Instruçao D.L. no. 7 de 3-2-1934. Educational Tax overprint. TIMOR, 1934.

Instruccion. 'Instruction' or 'Teaching'. Fiscals valid for postage. VENEZUELA.

Insufficiently Prepaid. Postage Due. No country name. ZANZIBAR, 1929–33.

Irian Barat. WEST IRIAN. Formerly Netherlands New Guinea and West New Guinea.

I.R. Official. Overprint on British stamps, 1882–1902. GREAT BRITAIN – Official Stamps (Inland Revenue).

Isla de Menorca. As part of overprint on stamps of Spain. SPAIN – Civil War issues (*Part 9*).

Island. ICELAND.

Islas Galapagos. GALAPAGOS ISLANDS.

Isole Italiani dell'Egeo. Overprint on Italian stamps. DODECANESE ISLANDS.

Isole Jonie. Overprint on Italian stamps. ITALIAN OCCUPATION OF IONIAN ISLANDS.

Istra. Overprint and surcharge on Italian stamps. VENEZIA GIULIA AND ISTRIA.

Itä-Karjala Sot. hallinto. Overprint on Finnish stamps. FINNISH OCCUPATION OF EASTERN KARELIA.

Italia/Poste Italiane. ITALY.

Jaffa. Overprint on stamps of Russia. RUSSIAN POST OFFICES IN THE TURKISH EMPIRE (*Part 10*).

Jam. Dim. Soomaaliya. SOMALIA, 1974–75.

Janina. Overprint and surcharge on Italian stamps. ITALIAN P.O.s IN THE TURKISH EMPIRE.

J.D. Soomaaliya. SOMALIA. 1976–77.

J.D. Soomaaliyeed. SOMALIA. 1977–.

Jeend (Jhind or **Jind) State.** Overprint on Indian stamps for JIND.

Jubilé de l'Union Postale Universelle. SWITZERLAND, 1900.

Jugoslavija. YUGOSLAVIA.

Julio 1936. Inscription on stamp of Spain. SPAIN – Civil War issues (*Part 9*).

K(ais). K(ön). Zeitungs-Stempel. 'Imperial/Royal Newspaper Stamp'. AUSTRIA or LOMBARDY AND VENETIA.

Kalayaan nang Pilipinas. JAPANESE OCCUPATION OF PHILIPPINES.

Kamerun. CAMEROUN. The former German colony.

Karabakh, Republic of Mountainous. NAGORNO-KARABAKH.

Karjala. KARELIA (*Part 10*).
Karki. Overprint on Italian stamps for Khalki. DODECANESE ISLANDS.
Karnten Abstimmung. Overprint on modified Austrian stamps for Carinthian plebiscite, 1920. AUSTRIA.
Karolinen. CAROLINE ISLANDS. The former German protectorate.
Kazahstan. KAZAKHSTAN.
Keneta. 'Cent' or 'cents'. HAWAII.

Kenttäpostia Fältpost. FINLAND – Military Field Post.
Kenya and Uganda. KENYA, UGANDA AND TANGANYIKA.
Kerassunde. Overprint on stamps of Russia. RUSSIAN POST OFFICES IN THE TURKISH EMPIRE (*Part 10*).
KGCA. Part of surcharge on Yugoslav Newspaper stamp for 1920 Carinthia Plebiscite. YUGOSLAVIA – Issues for Slovenia.
Kgl. Post. Frm. See 'Frimaerke Kgl'.
Kibris Türk Yonetimi/Kibris Türk Federe Devleti Postalari. CYPRUS (TURKISH CYPRIOT POSTS).
Kizilay Dernegi. (Red Crescent). Inscription on Obligatory Tax stamps of TURKEY.
K.K. Post-Stempel. 'Imperial/Royal Postage Stamp'. AUSTRIA (denominated in Kreuzer); LOMBARDY AND VENETIA (denominated in centes).

Klaipeda. Overprint, surcharge or inscription for MEMEL – Lithuanian Occupation.
Korea/Republic of Korea. KOREA (SOUTH KOREA).

Kosovo, United Nations Interim Administration in. UNITED NATIONS – Kosovo.
Kraljevstvo (or **Kraljevina**) **Srba, Hrvata i Slovenaca.** YUGOSLAVIA,1921–31.
K.S.A. Kingdom of SAUDI ARABIA. Stamps so inscribed 1975–82, since when inscription in Arabic only. Stamps identifiable by palm tree and crossed swords emblem.
K.u.K. Feldpost. 'Imperial and Royal Field Post'. AUSTRO-HUNGARIAN MILITARY POST.
K.u.K. Milit. Verwaltung Montenegro. Overprint on K.u.K. Feldpost stamps for the AUSTRO-HUNGARIAN MILITARY POST – Montenegro issues.
K.u.K. Militärpost. BOSNIA AND HERZEGOVINA. Austro-Hungarian Military Post.
Kurland. Overprint/surcharge on stamps of Germany. GERMAN OCCUPATION ISSUES, 1939–45 – Latvia (Courland) (*Part 7*).
Kuzey Kibris Türk Cumhuriyeti. CYPRUS (TURKISH CYPRIOT POSTS), since 1983.
K. Wurtt. Post. WURTTEMBERG.

La Canea. Overprint and surcharge on Italian stamps. ITALIAN P.O.s IN CRETE.
La Guaira. VENEZUELA – La Guaira (*Part 20*).
Läibäch, Provinz. Overprint/surcharge on stamps of Italy or inscription. SLOVENIA – German Occupation, 1943–45.
Land-Post Porto-Marke. BADEN – Rural Postage Due Samps.
LANSA (Lineas Aéreas Nacionales Sociedad Anonima). COLOMBIA – Private Air Companies.
Lao (**Postes**). LAOS since 1976.
L.A.R. 'Libyan Arab Republic'. LIBYA, 1969–77.
Lattaquie. Overprint on Syrian stamps for LATAKIA (formerly Alaouites).
Latvija (or **Latwija**). LATVIA.
Latvija 1941·I·VII. Overprint on Russian stamps for GERMAN OCCUPATION OF LATVIA.
Latvijas Aizsargi. 'Latvian Militia'. Overprint and surcharge. LATVIA.
Latvijas PSR. Issue inscribed for absorption of Latvia by Soviet Union, 1940. LATVIA.

Saudi Arabia

Libya

Slovenia

Latvia

Lebanon

Lithuania

North West Russia

Spanish Morocco

Lero or **Leros**. Overprint on Italian stamps for Leros. DODECANESE ISLANDS.

Levant. Overprint on British stamps for Middle East post offices. BRITISH LEVANT. Also overprint on Polish stamps for POLISH P.O. IN TURKEY.

Levante. Overprint and surcharge on Italian Express Letter stamps. ITALIAN P.O.s IN THE TURKISH EMPIRE.

Liban/République Libanaise. LEBANON.

Libia or **Libye**. LYBIA.

Libra. (Unit of weight). SPAIN – Official Stamps.

Lietuva or **Lietuvos**. LITHUANIA.

Lignes Aeriennes F.A.F.L. Overprint and surcharge on Syrian Air stamps of 1931. FREE FRENCH FORCES IN THE LEVANT, 1942.

Lima. Inscription and overprint on early issues of PERU (Lima is the capital).

Limbagan 1593–1943. Overprint on stamp of Philippines. JAPANESE OCCUPATION OF PHILIPPINES.

Linja Autorahti Bussfrakt. FINLAND – Parcel Post Stamps.

Lipso or **Lisso**. Overprint on Italian stamps for Lipso. DODECANESE ISLANDS.

Litwa Srodkowa. CENTRAL LITHUANIA. Independence issues of 1920–22.

L. Marques. Overprint on Mozambique stamps for LOURENCO MARQUES.

Logroño. As part of overprint on stamps of Spain. SPAIN – Civil War issues (*Part 9*).

Lokalbref. Local issue for Stockholm. SWEDEN (*Part 11*).

Lösen. Inscription on postage due stamps for SWEDEN, 1874.

Lothringen. Overprint on German stamps for GERMAN OCCUPATION OF LORRAINE, 1940.

LP 'Latwija Pashparwalac' (Independent Latvia) and cross of Russia. NORTH WEST RUSSIA.

Lubiana, R. Commissariato Civile, etc. Overprint on Yugoslav stamps for the Italian Occupation of SLOVENIA.

Luftfeldpost. Inscription on Nazi Air stamp of 1942. GERMANY – Military Fieldpost.

Macau. MACAO.

Madagascar, British Inland Mail. MADAGASCAR (*Part 1*).

Mafia, G.R. Post. Overprint on Indian Expeditionary Force stamps for TANGANYIKA – British Occupation, 1915.

Magyar Kir. Posta/Magyar Posta/Magyarország. HUNGARY.

Makedonija. MACEDONIA.

Malgache, République/Malagasy, Repoblika. MALAGASY REPUBLIC.

Malmédy. See Eupen & Malmedy.

Marianen. Inscription and overprint on German stamps for the MARIANA ISLANDS.

Maroc. FRENCH MOROCCO.

Maroc, Royaume du. 'Kingdom of Morocco'. MOROCCO.

Marocco or **Marokko**. Overprint and surcharge on German stamps for GERMAN P.O.s IN MOROCCO.

Marruecos, etc. SPANISH MOROCCO, SPANISH P.O.s IN TANGIER.

Marschall (or **Marshall**) **Inseln**. MARSHALL ISLANDS.

Mauritanie. MAURITANIA.

M.B.D. in oval. Overprint for Official stamps of NANDGAON.

Mecklenb. Schwerin. MECKLENBURG-SCHWERIN.

Mecklenb. Strelitz. MECKLENBURG-STRELITZ.

Mecklenburg-Vorpomm(ern). Mecklenburg-Vorpommern. ALLIED OCCUPATION OF GERMANY – Russian Zone (*Part 7*).

Medellin. ANTIOQUIA (Colombia). Issue of 1888.

M.E.F. 'Middle East Forces'. Overprint on British stamps. BRITISH OCCUPATION OF ITALIAN COLONIES.

Mejico, Correos. MEXICO. Issues of 1856 and 1864.

Melaka Malaysia. MALACCA. Issues from 1965.

Memelgebiet. Overprint and surcharge on German stamps for MEMEL.

Memento Avdere Semper L1 Bvccari. Surcharge on Yugoslav stamp. FIUME AND KUPA ZONE.

Metelin. Overprint on stamps of Russia. RUSSIAN POST OFFICES IN THE TURKISH EMPIRE (*Part 10*).

Militärpost Eilmarke. BOSNIA AND HERZEGOVINA – Newspaper Stamps.

Militärpost Portomarke. BOSNIA AND HERZEGOVINA – Postage Due Stamps.

Milliemes/Mill. Surcharges on French Colonial stamps. ALEXANDRIA AND PORT SAID.

Moçambique. MOZAMBIQUE.

Moçambique, Companhia (or **Comp.**) **de.** MOZAMBIQUE COMPANY.

Modonensi, Provincie. MODENA.

Monrovia. Registration stamp of LIBERIA, 1893.

Mont-Athos. Overprint on stamps of Russia. RUSSIAN POST OFFICES IN THE TURKISH EMPIRE (*Part 10*).

Montevideo. URUGUAY. Issues of 1858–59 and Air stamp of 1925.

Moyen Congo. MIDDLE CONGO.

MQE. Surcharge on French Colonies 'Commerce' type for MARTINIQUE.

M.V.i.R. Within frame. 'Militärverwaltung in Rumänien' (Military Administration in Romania). Overprint/surcharge in 'bani' on German stamps for the GERMAN OCCUPATION OF ROMANIA.

Nandgan. NANDGAON.

Napoletana, Bollo della Posta. NAPLES.

Nationaler Verwaltungsausschus 10·XI·1943. Overprint on Italian occupation stamps for MONTENEGRO – German Occupation.

Nations Unies. UNITED NATIONS – Geneva Headquarters. Overprint/inscription on Swiss stamps (1950–63). SWITZERLAND – International Organizations.

Naxçivan Poçt. NAKHICHEVAN.

N.C.E. or **N.-C.E.** Overprint/surcharge on French Colonies stamps for NEW CALEDONIA.

Negeri Sembilan. NEGRI SEMBILAN. Malaysia.

Nederland. NETHERLANDS.

Nederlands (or **Ned.**) **Nieuw-Guinea.** NETHERLANDS NEW GUINEA.

Nederlandsch (Ned. or **Nederl) Indië.** NETHERLANDS INDIES.

Nederlandse (or **Ned.**) **Antillen.** NETHERLANDS ANTILLES.

Nepriklausoma Lietuva 1941·VI·23. Overprint on Russian stamps for GERMAN OCCUPATION OF LITHUANIA.

Nezavisna Drzava (or **N.D.**) **Hrvatska.** Inscription or overprint on Yugoslav stamps for CROATIA.

N.F. Overprint on Nyasaland stamps for Nyasa-Rhodesian Force during British Occupation of TANGANYIKA, 1916. Sometimes erroneously ascribed to '(Gen.) Northey's Force'.

Nieuwe Republiek. NEW REPUBLIC. South Africa.

Nippon. JAPAN.

Nisiro or **Nisiros.** Overprint on Italian stamps for Nisiros. DODECANESE ISLANDS.

Nlle. Caledonie. Inscription or overprint on French stamps. NEW CALEDONIA.

Norddeutscher Postbezirk. NORTH GERMAN CONFEDERATION.

Norge/Noreg. NORWAY.

Nouvelle (or **Nlle.**) **Caledonie et Dependances.** NEW CALEDONIA.

Nouvelles Hebrides, Condominium des. NEW HEBRIDES.

NP. 'Naye paise' (Indian currency). Surcharge on British stamps for BRITISH POSTAL AGENCIES IN EASTERN ARABIA.

United Nations – Geneva Headquarters

Netherlands

Netherlands Indies

Norway

British Postal Agencies in Eastern Arabia

New Zealand – Life Insurance stamp

Norway – Official stamp

Jubaland

Syria

NSB. Overprint/surcharge on French Colonies stamps for NOSSI-BE.
N. Sembilan. NEGRI SEMBILAN. Malaysia.
N.S.W. NEW SOUTH WALES.
Nueva Granada, etc. See Estados Unidos.
N.W. Pacific Islands. 'North-West Pacific Islands'. Overprint on Australian stamps. NEW GUINEA.
N.Z. Inscription on Postage Due stamps (1899), Express Delivery stamp (1903) and Life Insurance Department stamps of NEW ZEALAND.

O.B. Overprint for 'Official Business' mail. PHILIPPINES.
Occupation Française. Overprint and surcharge on Hungarian stamps for FRENCH OCCUPATION OF HUNGARY – Arad.
Océanie. OCEANIC SETTLEMENTS.
Oesterreich(ische)/Oesterr. Post. AUSTRIA.
O.F. Castellorisio. 'Occupation Française'. Overprint on French stamps for occupation of CASTELROSSO.
Offentlig Sak/Off. Sak./O.S. Official stamps of NORWAY.
Office des Postes et Telecommunications. FRENCH WEST AFRICA.
Official. Overprint or inscription on stamps for use by government departments, e.g. BRITISH GUIANA, NEW ZEALAND.
O.H.M.S. 'On His/Her Majesty's Service'. Overprint on stamps for government use, e.g. CANADA, COOK ISLANDS, MONTSERRAT, NIUE (**O.K.G.S.** KIRIBATI).
Oil Rivers, British Protectorate. Overprint/surcharge on British stamps for Oil Rivers Protectorate. NIGER COAST PROTECTORATE.
Olsztyn Allenstein. Overprint on stamps of Germany. ALLENSTEIN.
Oltre Giuba. JUBALAND.
O.M.F. Cilicie. 'Occupation Militaire Française'. Overprint/surcharge on French stamps for French Military Occupation of CILICIA. Also, in full, on Turkish fiscal stamps.
O.M.F. Syrie. 'Occupation Militaire Française'. Overprint/surcharge on French stamps for French Military Occupation of SYRIA.

O.N.F. (or **B.N.F.**) **Castellorizo.** 'Occupation (or Base) Navale Française'. Overprint/surcharge on French/French Levant stamps for French Occupation of CASTELROSSO.
Onza. (Unit of weight). SPAIN – Official Stamps.
O.P.S.O. 'On Public Service Only'. Overprint on NEW ZEALAND stamps, 1891–1906.
Orange River Colony. Overprint on Cape of Good Hope stamps, or inscription, for ORANGE FREE STATE.
Oranje Vrij Staat. ORANGE FREE STATE.
Organisation Internationale pour les Réfugiés. 'International Refugees Organisation'. Overprint on Swiss stamps. SWITZERLAND – International Organizations.
Organisation Météorologique Mondiale. 'World Meteorological Organization'. Inscription on Swiss stamps. SWITZERLAND – International Organizations.
Organisation Mondiale de la Propriete Intellectuelle. 'World Intellectual Property Organization'. Inscription on Swiss stamps. SWITZERLAND – International Organizations.

Organisation Modiale de la Santé. 'World Heath Organisation'. Overprint/inscription on Swiss stamps. SWITZERLAND – International Organizations.
Orts-Post. 'Local Post'. SWITZERLAND, 1850.
O.S. Overprint on Australian stamps. AUSTRALIA – Official Stamps. Also PAPUA, TRINIDAD. Also see 'Offentlig Sak', etc.
O.S.G.S. 'On Sudan Government Service'. Overprint on Sudanese stamps. SUDAN – Official Stamps.

Österreich(ische). AUSTRIA.
Ostland. Overprint on German stamps for GERMAN OCCUPATION OF RUSSIA, 1941.
Ottomanes, Postes. TURKEY, 1914.
Oubangui-Chari/Oubangui-Chari-Tchad. UBANGI-SHARI.
O.V.S. 'Oranje Vrij Staat'. Inscription on Military Frank and Police Frank stamps of ORANGE FREE STATE.
O.W. Official. Overprint on British stamps. GREAT BRITAIN – Official Stamps (Office of Works).
O'zbekiston. UZBEKISTAN,

P (in oval with crescent and star). Overprint on Straits Settlements stamp. PERAK.
Pacchi Postali. 'Parcel Post'. ITALY. Also, inscribed 'R.S. Marino', SAN MARINO.
Packhoi. Overprint and Chinese surcharge on Indo-Chinese stamps for PAKHOI.
Pakke-Porto. 'Parcel Post'. GREENLAND.
Palestine. Overprint on E.E.F. stamps of PALESTINE. Overprint on Egyptian stamps. GAZA – Egyptian Occupation.
Para(s). Currency inscription on first issues of EGYPT. Also surcharge on stamps for AUSTRIAN P.O.s IN TURKEY, BRITISH LEVANT, FRENCH LEVANT, GERMAN P.O.s IN TURKEY, ITALIAN P.O.s IN THE TURKISH EMPIRE, ROMANIAN P.O.s IN THE TURKISH EMPIRE, RUSSIAN P.O.s IN THE TURKISH EMPIRE.
Parm, Stati, Parma, Duc. di or **Parmensi, Stati**. PARMA.
Parlamento a Cervantes, El. Cervantes commemorative. Official stamps of SPAIN, 1916.
Patmo or **Patmos**. Overprint on Italian stamps for Patmos. DODECANESE ISLANDS.

P D and numeral. 'Payé à Destination'. Overprint on plain paper. ST PIERRE ET MIQUELON (*Part 6*).
Pechino. Overprint/surcharge on Italian stamps for Peking. ITALIAN P.O.s IN CHINA.
Pentru Cultura. Inscription on Postal Tax stamps of ROMANIA, 1932.
Persanes, Postes. IRAN. Formerly 'Persia'.
Persekutuan Tanah Melayu. MALAYAN FEDERATION.
Peruana, Republica. PERU.
Pesa. Surcharge on German stamps for GERMAN EAST AFRICA.
Peseta(s). Surcharge on French stamps for FRENCH P.O.s IN MOROCCO.
P.G.S. 'Perak Government Service'. Overprint on Straits Settlements stamps. PERAK – Official Stamps.
Piaster. Surcharge on Austrian stamps for AUSTRIAN P.O.s IN THE TURKISH EMPIRE. Also on German stamps for GERMAN P.O.s IN THE TURKISH EMPIRE.
Piastra. Surcharge on Italian stamp. ITALIAN P.O.s IN CRETE.
Piastre(s). Surcharge on stamps for BRITISH LEVANT, FRENCH LEVANT, ITALIAN P.O.s IN THE TURKISH EMPIRE, RUSSIAN P.O.s IN THE TURKISH EMPIRE.
Pilgrim Tercentenary. Inscription on UNITED STATES commemorative set of 1920.
Pilipinas. PHILIPPINES. Inscription since 1962.
Pilipinas, Republika ng. JAPANESE OCCUPATION OF THE PHILIPPINES.
Piscopi. Overprint on Italian stamps for Tilos (Piskopi). DODECANESE ISLANDS.
Plebiscite Olsztyn Allenstein. Overprint on German stamps for plebiscite in ALLENSTEIN, 1920.
Pohjois Inkeri. NORTH INGERMANLAND. Part of Russia.
Polska/Poczta Polska. POLAND.
Polynesie Française. FRENCH POLYNESIA.
Porteado Correio. PORTUGAL – Postage Due Stamps.
Porte de Mar. MEXICO (*Part 15*).
Porte Franco. PERU.
Port Gdansk. Overprint on Polish stamps for POLISH POST IN DANZIG.

German Occupation of Russia

French Levant

Malayan Federation

British Levant

Great Britain – Postage Due

Ireland – Postage Due

Peru – Obligatory Tax stamp

Spain

Slovenia

Porte Franco. Inscription on early issues of PERU.

Porto Gazetei (Moldavian 'Bulls') or **Porto Scrisorei.** Earliest issues of ROMANIA.

Porto Rico. Overprint on U.S. stamps. PUERTO RICO – US OCCUPATION.

Portuguesa, Republica. PORTUGAL.

Portzegel. Overprint and surcharge for Postage Dues. NETHERLANDS.

Postage Due. No country name. GREAT BRITAIN or AUSTRALIA.

Postal Charges. Overprint for Postage Due stamps. PAPUA NEW GUINEA.

Post & Receipt or **Post Stamp.** Inscriptions on 'annas' stamps of HYDERABAD.

Postas le híoc. IRELAND – Postage Dues.

Poste Khedivie e Giziane/Postes Egyptiennes. EGYPT, 1872–88.

Poste Locale. SWITZERLAND – Transitional Period (*Part 8*) or Federal Administration.

Postgebeit Ob. Ost. Overprint on stamps of Germany. GERMAN COMMANDS.

Postzegel. Inscription on first issues of NETHERLANDS.

P.P. in box. Overprint on French Postage Due stamps. FRENCH MOROCCO.

Preussen. PRUSSIA.

P.R.G. 'People's Revolutionary Government', overprint on stamps of GRENADA for official use, 1982. Also Grenadines.

Pro Juventute. 'For the Children'. Charity stamps of SWITZERLAND.

Pro Patria. 'For the Fatherland'. National culture fund stamps of SWITZERLAND.

Pro (Plebiscito) Tacna y Arica. Obligatory Tax stamps of PERU, 1927–28.

Protectorado Español en Marruecos. SPANISH MOROCCO.

Protectorat Français. Overprint on French 'Maroc' key-types for FRENCH MOROCCO.

Pro Tuberculosis Probres. Inscription on stamp of SPAIN, 1937.

Pro Union Iberoamericana. Inscription on stamps of SPAIN, 1930.

Provinz Laibach/Ljubljanska Pokrajina. Inscription/overprint on Italian stamps for German Occupation of SLOVENIA.

Pto. Rico. PUERTO RICO.

P S N C (one letter in each in corner). 'Pacific Steam Navigation Company'. Provisional issue of PERU (*Part 20*).

Pulau Pinang Malaysia. PENANG. Issues from 1965.

Puolustusvoimat Kenttäpostia. FINLAND – Military Field Post.

Puttialla State. Overprint on Indian stamps for first issues of PATIALA.

R. Overprint/surcharge on French Colonies stamps for REUNION, 1885.

Raj Shahpura. SHAHPURA.

Rarotonga. Overprint/surcharge on New Zealand stamps, also inscription. COOK ISLANDS.

Rayon. SWITZERLAND, 1850–54.

Recargo/Recargo Transitorio de Guerra. SPAIN – War Tax Stamps.

Recuerdo del 1 de Febrero 1916 and portrait of Francisco Bertrand. HONDURAS.

Regatul Romaniei. Overprint with values in bani, leu or lei on Hungarian stamps for ROMANIA – Transylvania, 1919.

Regno d'Italia Trentino 3 nov 1918/Venezia Giulia 3·XI·18. Overprint on Austrian stamps. AUSTRIAN TERRITORIES ACQUIRED BY ITALY.

Reichspost. GERMANY. Empire issues, 1889–1901.

R.E.P. (or **Republika**) **Shqiptare.**
ALBANIA, 1925–30, 1939–43.
Repub. Franc. (Republique Française).
Abbreviation on early stamps of
FRANCE and FRENCH
COLONIES.
Repubblica Sociale (or **Rep. Soc.**)
Italiana. Overprint on stamps of
Italy. ITALY – Italian Social
Republic.
Républica Oriental. URUGUAY.
Republika Popullore e or **R.P.S.E.**
Shqiperise. ALBANIA, 1946–91.
République Française. FRANCE,
FRENCH COLONIES.
République Khmere. KHMER
REPUBLIC. Cambodia, 1971–75.
Retymno. Rethymnon Province –
RUSSIAN POST OFFICES IN
CRETE.
R.F. 'République Française'. FRANCE,
FRENCH COLONIES.
R.H. 'République d'Haiti'. Abbreviation
on Postage Due stamps. HAITI, 1898.
R.H. Official. Overprint on British
stamps. GREAT BRITAIN – Official
Stamps (Royal Household).
Rheinland-Pfalz. GERMANY. Allied
Occupation, 1947–49.
Rialtar Sealadac na Héireann 1922.
'Provisional Government of Ireland'.
Overprint on British stamps for
IRELAND (REPUBLIC).
Rizeh. Overprint on stamps of Russia.
RUSSIAN POST OFFICES IN THE
TURKISH EMPIRE (*Part 10*).
R.O. Overprint on stamps of Turkey.
EASTERN ROUMELIA AND
SOUTH BULGARIA.
Robertsport. Registration stamp of
LIBERIA, 1893.

Rodi. Overprint on Italian stamps, or
inscription, for Rhodes.
DODECANESE ISLANDS.
Romagne, Franco Bollo Postale.
ROMAGNA.
Romana/Romina. ROMANIA.
Rossija. RUSSIA – Russian Federation.

Roumelie Orientale. Overprint on
stamps of Turkey, or inscription.
EASTERN ROUMELIA AND
SOUTH BULGARIA.
Royaume de l'Arabie Soudite (or
Saoudite). SAUDI ARABIA.
R P SH. 'Republika Popullore e
Shqiperise'. On stamp depicting dove
with olive branch. ALBANIA.
RSA. 'Republic of South Africa'.
SOUTH AFRICA.
R.S.M. 'Repubblica di San Marino'.
SAN MARINO.
Ruanda. Overprint on stamps of
Belgian Congo. RUANDA-
URUNDI.
Rumänien. Overprint and value in
'bani' surcharged on German stamps.
GERMAN OCCUPATION OF
ROMANIA.
Rupee(s). Surcharge on British stamps
for BRITISH POSTAL AGENCIES
IN EASTERN ARABIA.
Russisch-Polen. Overprint on German
stamps for GERMAN
OCCUPATION OF POLAND.
Rwandaise, République. RWANDA,
1962–76.
Ryukus. RYUKU ISLANDS.

S. Overprint on Straits Settlements 2c.
stamp for SELANGOR, 1882.
S.A. SAUDI ARABIA.
Saargebeit/Saarland. SAAR. Now part
of Germany.
Sachsen. SAXONY.
Sachsen, Bundesland. East Saxony.
ALLIED OCCUPATION OF
GERMANY – Russian Zone
(*Part 7*).
Sachsen, Provinz. Saxony. ALLIED
OCCUPATION OF GERMANY –
Russian Zone (*Part 7*).
Sahara Español. SPANISH SAHARA.
**Sahara Occidental, Posesiones
Españolas del.** SPANISH SAHARA.
Salonicco. Overprint/surcharge on
Italian stamps for Salonika
(Thessaloniki). ITALIAN P.O.s IN
THE TURKISH EMPIRE.
Salonique. Overprint on stamps of
Russia. RUSSIAN POST OFFICES
IN THE TURKISH EMPIRE
(*Part 10*).
Salvador. EL SALVADOR.
Samoa i Sisifo. SAMOA.
Sandjak d'Alexandrette.
Overprint/surcharge on Syrian
stamps. ALEXANDRETTA.

France

South Africa

Saar

*Allied Occupation of
Germany*

Serbia

Albania

Thailand

Slovakia

Saorstát Eireann 1922. 'Irish Free State'. Overprint on British stamps for IRELAND (REPUBLIC).

S.A.R. 'Syrian Arab Republic'. SYRIA.

Sarkari. Overprint on Official stamps of SORUTH.

Sarre. Overprint on stamps of Germany and Bavaria. SAAR.

Saurashtra. SORUTH (Indian state).

Scarpanto. Overprint on Italian stamps for Karpathos. DODECANESE ISLANDS.

Scinde District Dawk. INDIA, 1852.

Scutari di Albania. Overprint/ surcharge on Italian stamps for ITALIAN P.O.s IN THE TURKISH EMPIRE.

Segnatasse. ITALY – Postage Due Stamps.

Sello 10°/25c. de Peso. Inscription on surcharged fiscal stamp. FERNANDO POO.

Senegambie et Niger. SENEGAMBIA AND NIGER.

Serbien. Overprint/surcharge on Yugoslav stamps for German Occupation of SERBIA; also overprint on Bosnian stamps for Serbian Issues of AUSTRO-HUNGARIAN MILITARY POST.

Sevilla. As part of overprint on stamps of Spain. SPAIN – Civil War issues (*Part 9*).

S H (one letter in each upper corner). SCHLESWIG-HOLSTEIN.

Shanghai China. Overprint/surcharge on U.S. stamps for UNITED STATES POSTAL AGENCY IN SHANGHAI.

Shqipenia. ALBANIA, 1913–20, 1995–.

Shqipenie. ALBANIA, 1920–22.

Shqiperia. ALBANIA, 1962–91.

Shqiperise. ALBANIA, 1948–62.

Shqipni. ALBANIA, 1937–38.

Shqipnija. ALBANIA, 1944, 1947.

Shqiptare. ALBANIA, 1991–95.

Shqyptare. ALBANIA, 1922–25, 1930.

Shri Lanka. SRI LANKA, issues of 1992–93.

S.H.S. 'Srba (Serbs), Hrvata (Croats), Slovena (Slovenes)'. Early issues of YUGOSLAVIA.

Siam. THAILAND, 1887–1939.

Sicilia, Bollo della Posta. SICILY.

Simi. Overprint on Italian stamps for Simi. DODECANESE ISLANDS.

Slesvig. SCHLESWIG. Plebiscite issues, 1920.

Slovenija. SLOVENIA.

Slovensko/Slovanska Posta. SLOVAKIA.

Slovenský Stat. Overprint on stamps of Czechoslovakia. SLOVAKIA.

Slova Posta. CZECHOSLOVAKIA – Postage Due stamps, 1919.

S. Marino, Repubblica (or **Rep.**) **di.** SAN MARINO.

Smirne. Overprint/surcharge on Italian stamps for Smyrna (Izmir). ITALIAN P.O.s IN THE TURKISH EMPIRE.

Smyrne. Overprint on stamps of Russia. RUSSIAN POST OFFICES IN THE TURKISH EMPIRE (*Part 10*).

S.O. 1920. 'Silesie Orientale'. Overprint on Czech and Polish stamps for EAST SILESIA.

Sobreporte. Special Fee stamp of COLOMBIA, 1865.

Socialist People's Libyan Arab Jamahiriya. LIBYA since 1977.

Sociedad Colombo-Alemana de Transportes Aéreos. Private Air Company stamps. SCADTA (*Part 20*), COLOMBIA (*Part 20*) and ECUADOR (*Part 20*).

Societé des Nations, also with **Courrier de la** or **Service de la**. Overprints on Swiss stamps for League of Nations. SWITZERLAND – International Organizations.

Soomaaliya (Soomaaliyeed or **Somaliya).** SOMALIA.

Soudan. Overprint on Egyptian stamps. SUDAN.

Soudan Français. FRENCH SUDAN.

South Georgia Dependency of. FALKAND ISLANDS DEPENDENCIES.

South Orkneys Dependency of. FALKAND ISLANDS DEPENDENCIES.

South Shetlands Dependency of. FALKAND ISLANDS DEPENDENCIES.

Sowjetische Besatszungs Zone. Overprint on German stamps for GERMANY (ALLIED OCCUPATION) – Russian Zone.

SPM or **St-Pierre M-on.** Overprint/surcharge on French Colonies stamps, or inscription. ST PIERRE ET MIQUELON.

Srbija i Crna Gora. SERBIA AND MONTENEGRO.

Srodkowa Litwa. CENTRAL LITHUANIA.

Stampalia. Overprint on Italian stamps for Astipalaia. DODECANESE ISLANDS.

S. Thomeé (or **Tomé**) **e Principe.** ST THOMAS AND PRINCE ISLANDS.

S.T. Trsta Vuja. TRIESTE – Zone B Yugoslav Military Government.

STT Vuja (or **Vujna**). Overprints on Yugoslav stamps. TRIESTE – Zone B Yugoslav Military Government.

Sud Kasai, Etat Autonome du. Overprint and inscription. SOUTH KASAI.

Sul Bolletino or **Sulla Ricevuta.** Inscriptions on left and right halves of Parcel Post stamps. ITALY. With star and crescent SOMALIA.

S.U./S. Ujong. SUNGEI UJONG.

Suidafrika (**Suid-Afrika** or **Republiek van Suid-Afrika**). SOUTH AFRICA.

Suidwes-Afrika. SOUTH WEST AFRICA.

Suomi. FINLAND.

Suriname. SURINAM.

Sverige. SWEDEN.

S.W.A. (or **SWA**). Overprints on South African stamps, also abbreviated inscription on stamps, for SOUTH WEST AFRICA.

Syrie/République Syrienne. SYRIA.

Syrie Grand Liban. Surcharge on French stamps. SYRIA – French Mandated Territory.

T with monetary unit in f(rancs). BELGIUM – Postage Due Stamps.

Tadzikistan. TAJIKISTAN.

Takse Pulu. Inscription on Postage Due stamps of TURKEY.

Tanganyika & Zanzibar, Republic of. TANZANIA.

Tanger. Overprint on French/French Morocco stamps for FRENCH P.O.s in TANGIER. Also overprint on Spanish stamps, or inscription, for SPANISH P.O.s IN TANGIER.

Tangier. Overprint on British stamps for MOROCCO AGENCIES – Tangier International Zone.

Tassa Gazette. MODENA – Newspaper Stamp.

Taxa de Guerra. War Tax surcharge. Distinguished by currencies. PORTUGUESE COLONIES ($), PORTUGUESE GUINEA (reis), PORTUGUESE INDIA (Rps), MACAO (avos).

Taxa Porto Pentru Cultura. Postal Tax Postage Due stamp of ROMANIA.

Te Betalen Port. Postage Due stamps of NETHERLANDS, CURAÇAO, SURINAM.

T.-C. Overprint on stamp of Cochin. TRAVANCORE-COCHIN.

T.C.E.K. 'Turkiye Cocuk Esirgeme Kurumu'. Inscription on Child Welfare stamps of TURKEY.

Tchad. CHAD.

T.C. Postalari. TURKEY.

T.E.O. 'Territoires Ennemis Occupés'. Overprint with surcharge in milliemes or piastres on French stamps for French Military Occupation of SYRIA. Also in paras on French Levant stamps for CILICIA.

T.E.O. Cilicie. Overprint on Turkish stamps for French Occupation of CILICIA.

Terres Australes et Antarctiques Françaises. FRENCH SOUTHERN AND ANTARCTIC TERRITORIES.

Territoire Français des Afars et des Issas. FRENCH TERRITORY OF THE AFARS AND THE ISSAS.

Territorios Espanoles del Golfo de Guinea. Inscription or overprint on Spanish stamps for SPANISH GUINEA.

Tetuan. Handstamp on Spanish stamps for SPANISH MOROCCO – Spanish P.O.s in Morocco.

South Africa

Sweden

South West Africa

French Southern and Antarctic Territories

Malaya – Thai Occupation

Tonga

Great Britain – Postage Due

Turkey

Thailand, with value in cents. MALAYA (THAI OCCUPATION).
Thirty Two Cents. With sailing ship. LIBERIA, 1886.
Thuringen. Thuringia. ALLIED OCCUPATION OF GERMANY – Russian Zone (*Part 7*).
Tientsin. Overprint/surcharge on Italian stamps for ITALIAN P.O.s IN CHINA.
Timor-Leste. EAST TIMOR.
Timor Lorosae. UNITED NATIONS – East Timor (UN Transitional Administration).
Tjeneste Frimaerke. DENMARK – Official Stamps.
Tjenestefrimerke. NORWAY – Official Stamps, 1925.
To Pay. No country name. GREAT BRITAIN – Postage Due Stamps.
Toga. TONGA, 1897–1944.
Togolaise, République. TOGO.
Toscano, Francobollo Postale. TUSCANY.
Touva. TUVA.
Traité de Versailles. Overprint on stamps of Germany. ALLENSTEIN.
Transjordan. JORDAN.
Trebizonde. Overprint on stamps of Russia. RUSSIAN POST OFFICES IN THE TURKISH EMPIRE (*Part 10*).
Trieste Trst in surcharge with date 1.V.1945 on Italian stamps. VENEZIA GIULIA AND ISTRIA – Yugoslav Occupation.
Tripoli di Barberia. Overprint on Italian stamps for ITALIAN P.O.s IN THE TURKISH EMPIRE.
Tripoli, Fiera Campionaria. On stamps inscribed Poste Italiane, R.R. Poste Coloniali or Posta Aerea with date 1935. TRIPOLITANIA. On stamps with dates 1936, 1937, 1938. LIBYA.
T.Ta.C. Inscription on Aviation Fund stamp of TURKEY.
T T T T. In corners of stamps with large numerals. DOMINICAN REPUBLIC – Postage Due Stamps.
Tunis, Tunisie or **République Tunisienne**. TUNISIA.
Türkiye Cumhuriyeti (or **T.C.**) **Postalari**. TURKEY.
Türkiye (or **Turk**) **Postalari**. TURKEY.
Türkmenpoçta. TURKMENISTAN.
Two Pence. Denomination on stamps showing Queen Victoria on throne. VICTORIA, 1852.

U.A.E. UNITED ARAB EMIRATES.

U.A.R. 'United Arab Republic'. Inscription on issues of EGYPT (value in milliemes), 1958–71, and SYRIA (value in piastres), 1958–61.
U.G. Typewritten inscription on first 'Missionary' stamps for UGANDA, 1895.
Ukraina. UKRAINE.
Ukraine. Overprint on German stamps for GERMAN OCCUPATION OF RUSSIA, 1941.
Ultramar. 'Beyond the Seas'. Inscription with year dates on stamps of CUBA, also overprinted for PUERTO RICO. Appears also on postal-fiscals of MACAO (values in avos) and PORTUGUESE GUINEA (values in reis).
UNEF. Overprint on Indian stamp for INDIAN U.N. FORCE IN GAZA (PALESTINE).
UN Force (India) Congo. Overprint on stamps of India, 1962. INDIAN U.N. FORCE IN CONGO.
Union Internationale des Télécommunications. 'International Telecommunications Union'. Inscription on Swiss stamps. SWITZERLAND – International Organizations.
Union Postale Universelle. 'Universal Postal Union'. Inscription on Swiss stamps. SWITZERLAND – International Organizations.
Union Postale Universelle, Jubile de l'. SWITZERLAND, 1900.
UNTEA. 'United Nations Temporary Executive Authority'. Overprint on stamps of Netherlands New Guinea for WEST NEW GUINEA.

Urundi. Overprint on stamps of Belgian Congo. RUANDA-URUNDI.

U.S. or **U.S.A.** UNITED STATES OF AMERICA.

U.S.T.C. Overprint on stamp of Cochin. TRAVANCORE-COCHIN.

Vallées d'Andorre. ANDORRA (French Post Offices), 1932–37.

Valona. Overprint/surcharge on Italian stamps. ITALIAN P.O.s IN THE TURKISH EMPIRE.

Vancouver Island. BRITISH COLOMBIA AND VANCOUVER ISLAND.

Van Diemen's Land. First issues of TASMANIA.

Vaticane, Poste. VATICAN CITY, to 1993. (Posta Aerea Vaticana – Air stamps).

Venezia Giulia. Overprint/surcharge on Italian stamps. AUSTRIAN TERRITORIES ACQUIRED BY ITALY.

Venezia Tridentina. Overprint/surcharge on Italian stamps. AUSTRIAN TERRITORIES ACQUIRED BY ITALY.

Vereinte Nationen. UNITED NATIONS – Vienna Centre.

VII Congreso U.P.U. Madrid 1920. Inscription on stamps of SPAIN.

VIII Världspost-Kongressen i Stockholm. SWEDEN, 1924.

Vilnius. Overprint on Russian stamps for GERMAN OCCUPATION OF LITHUANIA.

Virgin Islands. BRITISH VIRGIN ISLANDS.

Viva España as part of overprint on stamps of Spain. SPAIN – Civil War issues (*Part 9*).

Vojna Uprava Jugoslavenske Armije. Overprint/surcharge on Yugoslav stamps for VENEZIA GIULIA AND ISTRIA – Yugoslav Military Government.

Vojenska Posta. CZECHOSLOVAK ARMY IN SIBERIA.

Vom Empfänger Einzuziehen. DANZIG – Postage Due Stamps.

Vom Empfänger Zahlbar. BAVARIA – Postage Due Stamps.

V R in top corners. FIJI.

V.R.I. 'Victoria Regina Imperatrix'. Overprint with values in British currency on stamps of ORANGE FREE STATE.

W or **West Australia.** WESTERN AUSTRALIA.

Wilayah Persekutuan. MALAYSIA – Federal Territory issues.

Wendenschen Kreises, Briefmarke des/Packenmarke des. WENDEN.

Western Samoa. SAMOA.

Württemberg. WURTTEMBERG. Independent Kingdom. Also GERMANY (ALLIED OCCUPATION).

Y.A.R. 'Yemen Arab Republic'. YEMEN.

Yemen PDR. YEMEN PEOPLE'S DEMOCRATIC REPUBLIC.

Yemen, Republic of. YEMEN REPUBLIC (Combined).

Yunnansen/Yunnanfou. Overprint/surcharge on Indo-Chinese stamps. YUNNANFU.

Z. Afr. Rep(ubliek). TRANSVAAL.

Zanzibar. Overprint/surcharge on French stamps for FRENCH P.O.s IN ZANZIBAR.

Zara. Overprint on Italian stamps. GERMANY OCCUPATION OF DALMATIA.

Zelaya, Dpto. NICARAGUA – Zelaya (*Part 15*).

Zeitungs Stempel. 'Newspaper Stamp'. AUSTRIA or LOMBARDY AND VENETIA.

Zil Eloigne Sesel Seychelles. 'Seychelles Outer Islands'. ZIL EL WANNYEN SESEL, 1980–82.

Zil Elwagne Sesel Seychelles. See above, 1982–84.

Zona de Ocupatie Romana in small oval. Overprint on Hungarian stamps for Debrecen. ROMANIAN OCCUPATION OF HUNGARY.

Zona Occupata Fiumano Kupa. Overprint on Yugoslav stamps. FIUME AND KUPA ZONE.

Zona (de) Protectorado Español/en Marruecos. SPANISH MOROCCO.

Zone Française. GERMANY (ALLIED OCCUPATION) – French Zone, 1945–46.

Zuid Afrika. SOUTH AFRICA.

Zuid Afrikaansche (or Z. Afr.) Republiek. TRANSVAAL.

Zuidwest Afrika. SOUTH WEST AFRICA.

Zurich, Local Taxe. Zurich. SWITZERLAND – Cantonal Administrations (*Part 8*).

United Nations – Vienna Centre

Czechoslovak Army in Siberia

Yemen Arab Republic

Germany – Allied Occupation

OTHER ALPHABETS AND SCRIPTS

The Greek Alphabet

Greek is one of the classic languages – its alphabet was 'borrowed' from the Phoenicians whose extinct Semitic language was allied to Carthaginian and akin to Hebrew, and was, perhaps, the first tongue written in an alphabet proper. The word 'alphabet' itself is derived from *alpha*, *beta*, the first two Greek letters. Greek stamps have the country name 'Hellas' expressed (in Greek), a word which can be spelled out from the table below as *Ellas*. In fact since 1966 the version 'Hellas' has been printed alongside the Greek characters on the stamps.

Left: Aerospresso Co issue of 1926
Below: Greek stamp marking the cession of the Ionian Islands

Top: The first Greek stamps showed Hermes
Above: Anti-Tuberculosis Fund

Look out for the distinctive currency inscription – 100 lepta = 1 drachma. *Lepta* (singular, *lepton*) is expressed in a word which looks like 'AENTA' (although the first letter is an inverted 'V'), while *drachmai* (plural) appears at first glance as 'APAXMAI', though again the first letter is a triangle, the equivalent for 'D'. Sometimes these words are abbreviated. You may encounter overprints on Greek stamps and once you have decoded them it should be an easy matter to locate them in the catalogue. *Ellenike Dioikesis* ('Greek Administration') may be found on the Greek stamps of 1912 (provisionals for Balkan territories), or the Greek Occupation of Albania in 1940. The initials *S.D.D.* adjoining a surcharge within a scroll can be pinpointed to the Greek Occupation of the Dodecanese Islands. Thrace suffered various occupations in 1920, and a typical overprint reads, when decoded, *Diokesis Dutikes Frakes* or 'Administration of Western Thrace'. Stamps for the Greek island of Crete bear the inscription KPHTH which translates as *Krete*.

Modern Greek stamp inscribed 'ΕΛΛΑΣ ΔΗΜΟΚΡΑΤΙΑ'

SIMPLIFIED GREEK TABLE
with English equivalents

Greek		English	Greek		English
A	α	A	Ξ	ξ	X
B	β	B	O	ο	O
Γ	γ	G	Π	π	P
Δ	δ	D	P	τ	R
E	ε	E	Σ	σ	S
Z	ζ	Z		ς	(final)
H	η	E	T	τ	T
Θ	θ	TH	Y	υ	U
I	ι	I	Φ	φ	F
K	κ	K	X	χ	KH
Λ	λ	L	Ψ	ψ	PS
M	μ	M	Ω	ω	O
N	ν	N			

Conventional English equivalents are given. The actual pronunciation of some letters differs in modern spoken Greek.

A list of inscriptions in the Greek alphabet as they appear on stamps.

ΒΟΗΘΕΙΤΕ ΤΟΝ. Inscription on Charity Tax stamps. GREECE.

ΔΙΟΙΚΗΣΙΣ ΔΥΤΙΚΗΣ ΘΡΑΚΗΣ or **Διοίκησις (Δυτικής) Θράκης**. 'Administration of (Western) Thrace'. Overprint on stamps of Greece. THRACE.

Β∗Δ. Overprint on stamps of Greece for Khios. GREECE – Balkan War Issues (*Part 4*).

ΕΛΛΑΣ 2-Χ-43 in box. Handstamp on stamps for the Italian Occupation of Ionian Islands. GERMAN OCCUPATION OF ZANTE.

ΕΛΛΑΣ, ΕΛΛΑC or **ΕΛΛ**. GREECE.

ΕΛΛ. ΔΙΟΙΚ. ΓΚΙΟΥΜΟΥ ΛΤΖΙΝΑΣ. Overprint/surcharge on stamps of Turkey. THRACE – Greek Occupation, 1913, Issue for Gumultsina (*Part 4*).

ΕΛΛΗΝΙΚΗ ΧΕΙΜΑΡΡΑ. EPIRUS (*Part 4*).

ΕΛΛΗΝΙΚΗ ΔΗΜΟΚΡΑΤΙΑ. GREECE.

ΕΛΛΗΝΙΚΗ ΔΙΟΙΚΗCΙC. Overprint on stamps of Greece. GREEK OCCUPATION OF ALBANIA.

ΕΛΛΗΝΙΚΗ ΔΙΟΙΚΗΣΙΣ. Overprint on stamps of Greece, 1912. GREECE. Also on stamps of Greece (Ikaria) and Bulgaria (Kavalla). GREECE – Balkan War Issues (*Part 4*).

ΕΛΛΗΝΙΚΗ ΔΙΟΙΚΗΣΙΣ ΔΕΔΕΑΓΑΤΣ. 'Greek Administration Dedeagtz'. THRACE – Greek Occupation, 1913. Issue for Dedeagatz (*Part 4*).

Ελληνική Κατοχή Μυτιλήνης. 'Greek Possession Mytilene'. Overprint on stamps of Turkey for Lesvos. GREECE – Balkan War Issues (*Part 4*).

ΕΝΑΡΙΘΜΟΝ ΓΡΑΜΜΑΤΟΣΗΜΟΝ. Postage Due. GREECE.

ΕΘΝΙΚΗ ΠΕΡΙΘΑΛΨΙΣ. Inscription on 1914 Charity Tax stamp. GREECE.

ΕΠΑΝΑΣΤΑΣΙΣ 1922. 'Revolution 1922'. Overprint on stamps of Crete (and Greece). GREECE.

ΗΠΕΙΡΟΣ. EPIRUS (*Part 4*).

ΙΚΑΡΙΑΣ. Ikaria. GREECE – Balkan War Issues (*Part 4*).

ΙΟΝΙΚΟΝ ΚΡΑΤΟΣ. IONIAN ISLANDS.

ΙΤΑΛΙΑΣ–ΕΛΛΑΔΟΣ–ΤΟΥΡΚΙΑΣ. Inscription on Aerospresso Co issue of 1926. GREECE.

ΚΟΙΝΟΝ ΝΗΣΙΩΤΩΝ. Island Committee for Union with Greece. DODECANESE ISLANDS (*Part 4*).

Κ. Π. Overprint on Fiscal stamps (inscribed ΧΑΡΤΟΣΗΜΟΝ) of GREECE.

ΚΡΗΤΗ. CRETE.

Λ(or **Λ**)**ΗΜΝΟΣ**. Overprint on stamps of Greece for Limnos. GREECE – Balkan War Issues (*Part 4*).

ΟΛΥΜΠ. ΑΓΩΥΕΣ or **ΟΛΥΜΠΙΑΚΟΙ ΑΓΩΝΕΣ**. Olympic Games issue of 1906. GREECE.

Π.Ι.Π. (P.I.P. 'Patriotic Charity League'). Overprint on Red Cross stamp. GREECE.

ΠΡΟΣΤΑΣΙΑ ΦΥΜΑΤΙΚΩΝ. Anti-Tuberculosis Fund. GREECE.

ΠΡΟΣΩΡΙΝΗ ΚΥΒΕΡΝΗΣΙΣ. CRETE – Revolutionary Assembly.

ΠΡΟΣΩΡΙΝΟΝ ΤΑΧΥΔΡΟΜΕΙΟΝ ΗΡΑΚΛΕΙΟΥ. Candia Province – BRITISH P.O.s IN CRETE.

ΡΕΘΥΜΝΗΣ. Rethymnon Province – RUSSIAN POST OFFICES IN CRETE.

ΣΑΜΟΥ. Samos. GREECE – Balkan War Issues (*Part 4*).

Σ.Δ.Δ. Overprint on stamps of Greece. Greek Military Administration. DODECANESE ISLANDS (*Part 4*).

Υπάτη Αρμοστεία Θράκης. 'High Commission of Thrace'. Overprint/ surcharge on stamps of Turkey. THRACE.

Greek Occupation of Albania

'Greek Administration'

Greek Postage Due

Epirus

Ikaria

Saint Cyril, creator of the Cyrillic alphabet, and his brother St Methodius depicted on a Bulgarian stamp of 1975

The Cyrillic Group

Cyril and his brother Methodius were 9th century saints, apostles of the Slavs and natives of Salonika (now Thessalonica). They worked as Christian missionaries among the Slav peoples, and it was in an effort to unify the Slavonic languages that Cyril, nicknamed 'the philosopher', created what became known as the Cyrillic alphabet, a modification of the Greek alphabet with marked individual characteristics, comprising 33 letters. Cyril set down his alphabet in AD 855, and it can be seen from the tables of Greek and Cyrillic letters that several Cyrillic characters are identical to those of the Greek alphabet: some, indeed, have the same English equivalents.

Despite these similarities the Cyrillic letters are quite distinctive and once you have familiarized yourself with the alphabet on page 33, you will be able to recognize a stamp's country name or inscription at sight. You will then know that the stamp belongs to Russia (or one of its former districts or regional governments and post offices) or to Mongolia, Yugoslavia (including the ancient kingdoms of Montenegro and Serbia), or Bulgaria, which was once the territory of a great empire.

RUSSIA

The language of the peoples of Central Russia – which is also the official and literary language of the Russian nation – has a great many dialects, but in the main these are phonetic variations. The basic Cyrillic alphabet is universal throughout the country. Prior to the Revolution of 1917, Russian stamps were simply inscribed *mapka*, which translates as 'marka' or 'stamp', or with a word which looks like *noyta*, meaning 'pochta' or 'post'. Clues to identification are also provided by the currency denominations – the word which looks like *kon* is easily decoded as 'kop', short for 'kopeck', the unit of Russian currency. A hundred kopecks equal one 'rouble', a word which again is abbreviated on Russian stamps – the word, which looks like *pye*, is decoded as 'roob' or 'rouble'. Immediately following the Revolution, Russian stamps bore an inscription which looked something like 'P.C.I.C.P.'. This is interpreted as 'R.S.F.S.R.', an abbreviation for the provisional country name of 'Russian Socialist Federal Soviet Republic'. From 1923 to 1991 Russian stamps were inscribed CCCP, which translates as 'SSSR', the initial letters for the four Russian words meaning 'Union of Soviet Socialist Republics' (*Soyuz Sovyetskikh Sotsialisticheskikh Respublik*), familiar to us as 'U.S.S.R.'. Also familiar on Russian stamps until 1991 was the word *noyta* which meant 'post'. Since 1991 the country name has also appeared in the western alphabet as 'ROSSIJA'.

Stamps were issued in Batum (or Batoum), a town in Georgia on the eastern shore of the Black Sea, in 1919 during the British occupation following the War of 1914–18, the inscription in the scroll at the top of the stamps translates to *Batoomskaya pochta*, which means 'Batum post'. Stamps issued for the Russian Post Offices in Turkey in 1868 and 1879 can be identified by the inscription around the value numeral which may be decoded as *Vostochnaya korrespondentsia* or 'Oriental correspondence'. The penultimate letter 'I' in this inscription is now obsolete.

Various anti-Bolshevik governments existed in Siberia for some years after the Revolution – the Cyrillic inscriptions and overprints are similar to those on Russian stamps and positive identification is best obtained by reference to the catalogue. South Russia also had temporary post-Revolution governments and here again reference to the catalogue illustrations is advised.

Stamps of Russia (left to right): Empire, Russian Socialist Federal Soviet Republic, Union of Soviet Socialist Republics and Russian Federation

The Ukraine is a vast territory of the U.S.S.R. which issued stamps during its temporary independence after the Revolution, between 1918 and 1923 and again from 1992. The 'trident' emblem on overprints and in designs is a clue to identity, while reference to the Cyrillic chart decodes the main inscription as *Ookrains'ka*, or Ukraine. For West Ukraine, Austrian stamps were overprinted with a trident in 1919 and letters which translate to *Z.Oo.N.R.*, meaning 'West Ukraine People's Republic'. Wenden, the 'Land of the Wends', now part of Latvia, issued its own stamps up to 1901 – the principal word in the inscription emerges as *Vendenskaya*. Earlier issues are inscribed in German – *Wendensche Kries Briefmarke*.

Russian stamps were overprinted/surcharged for Armenia – mostly new-value surcharges and distinctive monogram devices; Georgia – surcharges, including the hammer and sickle, in 1923; and for the Russian Post Offices in China – note that the overprinted country name (which looks like the Greek name for 'Crete'), which translates as *Kitai*, is the Russian word for 'China'. Mongolia, the republic in Central Asia located between Russia and China, is largely under Russian influence.

The Mongolian language used to be written in a vertical script and this is found on early stamps; the Cyrillic alphabet was introduced on stamps in 1943 and has continued since. The common inscription translates as *Mongol shoodan*, or 'Mongolian post', while the Cyrillic initials *BNMAU* stand for 'All-in-agreement Mongol People's Country'. Mongolian stamps from 1959 have been additionally inscribed 'Mongolia' in the normal alphabet, thus making identification an easy matter.

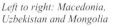

Ukraine

Left to right: Macedonia, Uzbekistan and Mongolia

The splitting of the former Soviet Union into separate states has resulted in new stamps from Russian Federation, Armenia, Azerbaijan, Belarus, Estonia, Georgia, Kazakhstan, Kyrgyzstan, Latvia, Lithuania, Moldovia, Tajikistan, Turkmenistan, Ukraine and Uzbekistan. The stamps of the three Baltic States and Moldovia are inscribed in the normal alphabet and Azerbaijan as 'Az3rbaycan'; Georgia has its own script. Most stamps of the other states are inscribed in both alphabets.

Yugoslavia

YUGOSLAVIA

The Socialist Federal Republic of Yugoslavia – the land of the southern Slavs – was proclaimed in 1945. It was, however, established in 1918 as the kingdom of the Serbs, Croats and Slovenes, comprising Montenegro, Serbia, Bosnia, Herzegovina and parts of pre-war Hungary, with separate stamp issues for the various states. In 1931, when the new country title of 'Jugoslavija' was officially adopted, definitive stamps appeared inscribed in Serbo-Croat (the *lingua franca* of Yugoslavia) and in the Cyrillic alphabet. Occasionally, since that time, Yugoslav stamps have been issued bearing only the Cyrillic inscription, but these are readily identifiable on reference to any of the dual-language stamps.

The former monarchy of Montenegro issued its own stamps from 1874 until 1913, and the country name – in Cyrillic characters – is rather misleading. It decodes in the native tongue as *Tsrna* (or *Tsr.*) *Gora*, or *Tsrne Gore* – in modern parlance, *Grna Gora*, in other words, Montenegro or 'Black mountain'. *Poshte* is another version of the word for 'post'. The former kingdom of Serbia first issued stamps in 1866 and used the Cyrillic alphabet consistently, even through the German occupation of 1941–43. The country name readily translates as *Srbija, Srbska* or *Srpska*. Note that the 'j' is one of the Serbian special letters. The word for 'post' is *poshta*, and the currency is another clue – 100 para equalling 1 dinar. The Cyrillic for 'para' looks like *napa*.

Serbia and Montenegro

The division of Yugoslavia in the 1990s has led to separate issues for Bosnia and Herzegovina, Croatia, Macedonia and Slovenia. Since 2003 the country has become Srbija i Crna Gora (Serbia and Montenegro), in normal or Cyrillic alphabets.

BULGARIA

A Balkan republic, Bulgaria adjoins the Black Sea on the east, and is bounded by Romania, Yugoslavia, Greece and Turkey. Formerly a Turkish province, it became a principality under Turkish suzerainty in 1878, Eastern Roumelia was incorporated with it in 1885. Bulgaria's first stamps were issued in 1879, establishing the country name in Cyrillic letters which can be deduced as 'B'lgariya' (the second letter is silent and is thus represented by an apostrophe). With the accession of Tsar Ferdinand in 1907, the word for 'kingdom' – 'Tsarstvo' – was added. The currency – 100 stotinki = 1 lev (plural, leva) – is also easily identified: 'stotinki' is expressed as 'ctot...'. After Bulgaria became a republic in 1946, until 1989, stamps bore the Cyrillic letters 'HP' before the country name, translated as 'NR' or 'Narodna Republika' or 'People's Republic'. Since 1989 Bulgarian stamps have also been inscribed 'Bulgaria'.

Some inscriptions in the Cyrillic alphabet as they appear on stamps.

Top: Kingdom of Bulgaria, an Express stamp of 1939
Above: A modern stamp of Bulgaria

А.С.С.Р. 'A.S.S.R' (Azerbaijan Soviet Socialist Republic). AZERBAIJAN.

АЭРБАИДЖАНСКАЯ. AZERBAIJAN.

АМЖРСКАЯ ОБЛСТИАЯ ПОЧТОВАЯ МАРКА. 'Amur Province Postage Stamp'. SIBERIA.

БАНЛЕРОЛЬНОЕ ОТПРАВЛЕНІЕ НА ВОСТОКЪ. 'Dispatch under wrapper to the East'. RUSSIAN POs IN THE TURKISH EMPIRE.

БАТУМСАЯ ПОЧТА, БАТУМ(Ъ) or **БАТУМ. ОБЛ.** BATUM.

БЪЛ(огЛ)ГАРИЯ. BULGARIA.

БЪЛГАРСКА. BULGARIA.

ВЕНДЕНКАЯ. WENDEN.

ВОСТОЧНАЯ КОРРЕСПОНДЕНЦІЯ. 'Eastern Correspondence'. RUSSIAN POs IN THE TURKISH EMPIRE.

В П26П V 1921–1922 in oval. Overprint on stamps of SIBERIA.

Г.С.С.Р. in circle with star 'G.S.S.R.' (Gorskaya Soviet Socialist Republic). Overprint on stamps of Russia. SOUTH RUSSIA (*Part 10*).

Д.В. Overprint on Russian stamps. SIBERIA.

ДРЖВА СХС. YUGOSLAVIA – Issues for Bosnia and Herzegovina.

ЕДИНАЯ РОССІЯ. SOUTH RUSSIA.

Э.А. and cross of Russia in circle. 'Zapadnaya Armiya' (Western Army). Overprint on stamps of Latvia. NORTH WEST RUSSIA.

ЗСФСР. TRANSCAUCASIAN FEDERATION.

З.У.Н.Р. Overprint in corners of Austrian stamps. WEST UKRAINE.

КАЗАКСТАН. KAZAKHSTAN.

КИТАЙ. Overprint on stamps of Russia. RUSSIAN POs IN CHINA.

КРАЉЕВСТВО СХС. YUGOSLAVIA – Issues for Bosnia and Herzegovina.

КРЫМСКАГО КРАЕВОГО ПРАВИТЕЛЬСТВА. 'Crimean Regional Government'. Inscription on postage and currency stamp. SOUTH RUSSIA.

К. С. or **К. СРБСКА ПОШТА.** SERBIA.

КЫРГЫЗСТАН. KYRGYSTAN.

КЊ. СРП. ПОШТА. SERBIA.

МАКЕДОНИЯ. Overprint on stamps of Bulgaria. MACEDONIA – German Occupation.

МАКЕДОНИЈА. MACEDONIA.

Н НА А В. П. П. Handstamp on stamps of Russia. SIBERIA (*Part 10*).

ОКСА. 'Osobiy Korpus Severnoy Armiy' (Special Corps Northern Army). NORTH WEST RUSSIA.

П.З.К. below three horizontal bars, all in frame. Handstamp on stamps of SIBERIA.

ПОЧТОВАЯ МАРКА. 'Postage Stamp'. Inscription on early stamps of FINLAND, RUSSIA, SERBIA, SIBERIA and SOUTH RUSSIA.

ПОШТЕЦРНЕГОЕ. MONTENEGRO.

ПОРТО СКРИСОРИ. ROMANIA – Moldavia.

Прпам. ЗЕМСКІЙ Край. 'Priam Zemskiye Kraye' (Primur Territory). SIBERIA.

Bulgarian Sunday Delivery stamp

ПЯТЬ. Overprint on stamps of Russia. SOUTH RUSSIA.

РЕРУБЛИКА СРПСКА КРАЈИНА. CROATIA – Serbian Posts (Republic of Srpska Krajina).

РЕПУБЛИКА СРПСА. 'Republika Srpska'. Serbian administration in BOSNIA AND HERZEGOVINA.

РОПИТ. 'Russian Company for Steam Shipping and Trade'. RUSSIAN POs IN THE TURKISH EMPIRE.

РОССІЯ. RUSSIA, SOUTH RUSSIA.

РСФСР. 'RSFSR' (Russian Socialist Federal Soviet Republic). RUSSIA.

РУССКОЙ АРМІИ. Overprint on stamps of Russia, South Russia and Russian POs in the Turkish Empire. RUSSIAN REFUGEES POST (*Part 10*).

СБЕРЕГАТЕЛЬНАЯ МАРКА. Inscription on Postal Savings Bank stamps authorised for postage. RUSSIA.

СРБИЈА. SERBIA.

СРЬИЈА И ЦОРА.'Serbia and Montenegro'. SERBIA.

СРЕМСКО-БАРАІЬСКА ОБЛАСТ. CROATIA – Serbian Posts (Sremsko Braanjska Oblast).

СССР. 'USSR' (Union of Soviet Socialist Republics). RUSSIA.

ТЬВА or **ТЫВА**. TUVA.

УКРАЇНСЬКА, УКРАЇНИ or **УКРАЇНА**. UKRAINE.

УКР. Н. Р. or **УКР. Н. РЕП.** Overprint on stamps of Austria, Austro-Hungarian Military Post and Bosnia and Herzegovina. WEST UKRAINE.

У.С.С.Р. UKRAINE.

ФОНД(Ъ) САНАТОРИУМЪ. 'Sanatorium Fund'. Inscription on Sunday Delivery stamps of BULGARIA.

ЦР. ГОРЕ, ЦРНЕ ГОРЕ or **ЦРНА ГОРЕ**. MONTENEGRO.

ЮГЪ РОССІИ. Overprint on stamps of Russia. SOUTH RUSSIA.

ЮЖНА БЪЛАРИЯ. Overprint on stamps of Bulgaria. EASTERN ROUMELIA AND SOUTH BULGARIA.

ЈУГОСЛАВИЈА. YUGOSLAVIA.

Batum

Finland (denominated in markka)

'China' overprint on Russia

Simplified decipherment table

Russian	English	Russian	English
А а	A	П п	P
Б б	B	Р р	R
В в	V	С с	S
Г г	G	Т т	T
Д д	D	У у	OO
Е е	E	Ф ф	F
Ё ё	YO	Х х	KH
Ж ж	ZH	Ц ц	TS
З з	Z	Ч ч	CH
И и	I	Ш ш	SH
Й й	I	Щ щ	SHCH
К к	K	Ъ ъ	(silent)
Л л	L	Ы ы	I
М м	M	Ь ь	(silent)
Н н	N	Э э	E
О о	O	Ю ю	YU
		Я я	YA

Other Cyrillic letters

Obsolete

І	і	I
Ѣ	ѣ	YE
Ѳ	ѳ	F
Ѵ	ѵ	I
Ѫ	ѫ	U

Ukrainian

Є	є	YE

Macedonian

Ѕ	ѕ	DZ

Serbian

Ђ	ђ	DJ
Ћ	ћ	C

Serbian and Macedonian

Ј	ј	J
Љ	љ	LJ
Њ	њ	NJ
Џ	џ	DZ

Mongolian

Ү	ү	Ü
Ө	ө	Ö*

*Obsolete letter revived with new sound

Serbia

Croatia – Serbian Posts (Srpska Krajina)

'Official' overprint on Indian stamp for the Convention State of Gwalior

Indian Native States

Prior to independence in 1947, India embraced numerous princely states, some of which issued stamps. For convenience, philatelists divide them into two groups – the so-called Convention States and the Indian Feudatory States. The Convention States, which, under a series of postal conventions established by the Imperial Government, used Indian stamps overprinted with their various names (usually in English and thus easily identified), were: Chamba; Faridkot after 1887; Gwalior; Jind (Jhind or Jeend) from 1885; Nabha; and Patiala (also spelled Puttialla). The exceptional overprint of Gwalior official stamps is illustrated. These stamps were valid for postage within the state of issue, to other Convention states and to destinations in British India.

Stamps in a wide variety of often primitive designs were issued by the Indian Feudatory States – these could only be used within the borders of their respective states. Some issues are extremely rare and the whole group has become quite popular with collectors seeking a novel and complex subject for philatelic study. Some typical designs are illustrated from each Feudatory State. With the exception of the 'Anchal' stamps of Travancore-Cochin (1951), all these stamps were replaced by those of the Republic of India on 1 May 1950.

INDIAN FEUDATORY STATES

Alwar   *Bahawalpur*   *Bamra*   *Barwani*   *Bhopal*

Bhor   *Bijawar*   *Bundi*   *Bussahir*

Charkhari   *Cochin*   *Dhar*   *Duttia*   *Faridkot pre-1887*

Hyderabad

Idar

Indore (Holkar)

Jaipur

Jammu & Kashmir

Jasdan

Jhalawar

Jind pre-1885

Kishangarh

Las Bela

Morvi

Nandgaon

Nawanagar

Orcha

Poonch

Rajasthan

Rajpipla

Sirmoor

Soruth

Travancore

Travancore-Cochin

Wadhwan

Far East Scripts
Some difficult stamps for the new collector to identify are those from the countries of the Far East – China, Japan, Manchukuo, Ryukyu Islands and North and South Korea. China is further complicated because of the several different governments which have been in control (on the mainland and on the island of Taiwan, also known as Formosa). Parts of China have also been occupied by the Japanese and there are innumerable overprints and surcharges among China's prolific stamp issues. A preliminary study of the historical notes and the illustrations listed under China in the catalogue is recommended.

CHINA
A distinguishing emblem – the twelve-rayed sun – was used on Chinese stamps in pre-Communist times (up to 1949): note that it was also used on stamps listed under the Japanese Occupation of China. In the Chinese language each character is a complete word: the various symbols are not letters of an alphabet. At one time the characters read downwards, one below the other, but nowadays sentences are more often written horizontally, though from right to left. In modern times – particularly under the Communist regime – the tendency is to write from left to right as in English. Look for the character *chung* (it is rather like a double-sided flag) at the beginning of the sentence (whether it is first or last) and count up to the third

Chinese provinces (from top): Kirin and Heilungkiang; Sinkiang, Szechwan and Yunnan

character – if it resembles a letter 'R' then the stamp is a pre-Communist issue. In the same location on stamps of the Communist People's Republic the character looks like an inverted 'V'. Most China (People's Republic) commemorative stamps have a serial number at the foot of the design, for example 'T. 108. (6-4) 1986'. This helps to aid rapid identification of Chinese issues. From 1992 People's Republic stamps have included the name 'CHINA' in the western alphabet.

The same rule applies to the stamps of Taiwan from 1949 – the birth of the Chinese Nationalist Republic. Modern Taiwan stamps are inscribed 'Republic of China'.

Above: Stamps of Imperial China (far left) and the Chinese Republic
Far left: Chinese People's Republic
Left: Taiwan (Republic of China)

Japan. Design with Chrysanthemum emblem, stamp with name in Japanese characters only and issue including the name 'Nippon'

JAPAN

Japanese is written in ideographic (picture-symbol) characters, acquired from China. Indeed, through constant contact with the Chinese people down the centuries (in peace and war), the Japanese language has enriched itself with Chinese words and expressions. Japanese stamps up to 1947 often had an emblem representing a chrysanthemum included in the design. And from 1966 the word 'Nippon' in our alphabet has been added to Japanese stamp designs. Inscriptions in the native language include the country name which comprises a standard group of four characters. The first of these (which may be last depending in which direction the sentence has been written) is easily recognizable – it resembles a box with a horizontal line through the middle.

In 1930 Japan alleged that her interests in Manchuria were being jeopardized by the Chinese and began the military occupation of the area, setting up a new puppet state of Manchukuo, consisting of the former provinces of Fegtien, Kirin, Heilungchiang and Jehol. Pu Yi, who later became Emperor Kang-teh (of *The Last Emperor* film fame), was appointed Head of State. The stamps, identified by the orchid crest and by the currency – 100 fen = 1 yuan – are listed in the catalogue under Manchukuo.

Japanese occupation of Malaya

RYUKYU ISLANDS

Ryukyu stamps, first issued in 1948, closely resembled those of Japan in style, inscriptions and currency – 100 sen = 1 yen. The main inscription, however, lacks the box-like character noted above for Japan. Under United States administration the stamps were issued in American cents and dollars from 1958 – note the distinctive '¢' for cents. From 1961 the word 'Ryukyus' appeared on the stamps, which ceased in 1972 when the islands were handed back to Japan.

Manchukuo

KOREA

The divided nation. Emblems and inscriptions help to distinguish the stamps of South and North Korea. Unlike Chinese, each sign in the Korean language is a separate letter of the alphabet – these are combined in groups to form complete characters. North Korean inscriptions have four such characters, those of South Korea have six, the first one resembling 'CH'. South Korean stamps additionally bear the *yin yang* symbol – a circle part light and part dark – and have been inscribed 'Republic of Korea' in English since 1966.

Ryukyu Islands

Korea. US Military Government surcharge on Japanese stamp, issues of South and North Korea

Other Scripts

Unfamiliar scripts and alphabets may present a problem if there is no other clue to a stamp's origins. Some are illustrated here as a general guide. Note the appearance and 'look' of an inscription, and observe particularly whether the script comprises separate characters (like the Amharic language from Ethiopia, or the Siamese language of Thailand which is derived from a form of Sanskrit and has affinities with Chinese), or in flowing style like Arabic or Persian, which is a version of Arabic. Most Arab countries inscribe their stamps additionally in English or French, but remember that Arabic is written from right to left and that there are six chief dialects – Algerian, Moroccan, Syrian, Egyptian, Iraqi and Arabian. The Turkish language, formerly written in Arabic characters, was changed to Roman by the order of Ataturk in 1928. Note also that Israel stamps, following the first 'Coins' issue of 1948, have been inscribed not only in Hebrew and Arabic, but in English as well.

Left to Right: Turkey, Afghanistan, Iran, Saudi Arabia

Malaya (Perak)

Some of the Malay States are easy to identify with the names shown in English – Johore, Kedah, Malacca (or Melaka), Penang (or Pulau Pinang) and Sungei Ujong. But some have the state's name only in Malay script – which looks all 'dots and dashes' and has Arabic elements: These include Kelantan, Negri Sembilan (or Negeri Sembilan), Pahang, Perak, Perlis, Selangor and Trengganu. Look for a similar sultan's portrait or state arms in the catalogue. The Afghan languages are Persian or Pushtu (or Pashtu), but the stamps are usually inscribed in French – Postes Afghanes – as well as the native script. Nepali is the spoken language of the Gurkha peoples of Nepal, but all except the earliest stamps have been additionally inscribed 'Nepal' in English. Burmese, the language of the people of Burma (now Myanmar), is allied to Chinese and is written in an alphabet derived from India, the characters of which are more or less circular and thereby easily identifiable on Burmese stamps in addition to the 'Burma Postage' or 'Union of Burma' inscriptions. The stamps of Sri Lanka (Ceylon) are unusual in that they are inscribed trilingually – Sinhalese, Tamil and English.

From far left: Different scripts on stamps of Georgia, Nepal, Burma and Tuva

'No-name' Stamps

As mentioned in the beginning of this book, Great Britain is the only country in the world whose stamps do not bear the name of the issuing country, although all of them bear the likeness of the ruling monarch. In early days – before the foundation of the Universal Postal Union, other countries sometimes did not include their names. Three stamps which apparently defied the U.P.U. convention were issued by the United States in 1920, marking the tercentenary of the Landing of the Pilgrim Fathers – they omitted the customary 'U.S. Postage'.

Some 'difficult' countries are listed below with a number of the stamps illustrated.

Austria. Check the currencies on early issues because, although the designs are similar, your stamps might be from Austrian Post Offices in Turkey, or from Lombardy and Venetia. The head of Mercury, messenger of the gods, appears on Austrian newspaper stamps.

Bahrain. Arabic inscription with 'key'-like word under circle – 1974 War Tax Stamp. (Also 1973 issue, without 'key'.)

Bosnia and Herzegovina. The Austrian coat-of-arms is prominent.

Brazil. The early 'numeral' stamps represented 'Bull's-eyes', 'Goat's-eyes' and 'Snake's-eyes' respectively. A 'Bull's-eye' is shown on page 5.

Finland. Circles in the designs distinguish the 1891 issue from the similar issues of Russia. Also issues between 1901 and 1911 bear the face value in Finnish *penni* and *markkaa*.

Emblems on stamps can also aid identification. Shown below are Yin yang (South Korea), Chrysanthemum (Japan), Orchid (Manchukuo), Star and crescent (Turkey, Pakistan, Bahawalpur, Hyderabad), Toughra (Turkey, Saudi Arabia, Afghanistan), Palm tree and crossed scimitars (Saudi Arabia) and Trident (Ukraine)

Alsace and Lorraine   *Austria*   *Austria – Postage Due*

Austria – Newspaper Stamps

Bahrain – War Tax   *Belgium*   *Bosnia and Herzegovina*

Hungary. 1871–88. Similar to Austria, but the designs are distinctive.
Papal States. The crossed keys are the main clue. Cf. First issue of Vatican City.
Portugal. 'Correio', the 'reis' currency and the Royal heads suggest Portugal.
Sardinia. Compare with very similar stamps of Italy, 1862.
Saudi Arabia. Palm tree emblem only on stamps from 1982.
Spain. Stamps with various portraits, often inscribed Communicaciones, sometimes dated, and with currencies in cuartos, centimos and pesetas, indicate 19th century Spain, but should be checked with contemporary issues of Cuba, Puerto Rico or the Philippines, particularly if the inscription includes Ultramar.
Switzerland. Early postage dues were unnamed, being regarded as of internal significance only.

Germany (Allied Occupation) –
Russian Zone, East Saxony (Part 7)   *Hungary*

Iran   *Netherlands*   *Papal States*   *Portugal*

Sardinia   *Spain*   *Switzerland – Postage Dues*

Not Malta or Greece, or even   *Venezuela*   *Yugoslavia, imperf versions*
Syria, but Vatican City!   *are Newspaper Stamps of*
                                                             Bosnia and Herzegovina